Praise for *Reclaim the Plot*

"In war and in organizations, failure rarely comes from a lack of intelligence—it comes from losing shared awareness. Reclaim the Plot *is a powerful reminder that leadership under complexity requires humility, trust, and distributed judgment. Kelly Monahan captures, with uncommon clarity, how organizations drift into failure—and how they can find their way back."*

—General (Ret) Stan McChrystal
Founder & CEO, McChrystal Group

"As work continues to evolve, leaders face difficult questions about how to organize teams, sustain productivity, and support employees effectively. Reclaim the Plot *offers a practical and readable framework for thinking through those challenges."*

—Nick Bloom
William Eberle Professor of Economics,
Stanford University

"Reclaim the Plot *is one of those rare leadership books that's both useful and genuinely engaging to read. Kelly Monahan blends relatable storytelling with clear, actionable insights that leaders can actually apply, especially in a moment when AI is rewriting the rules of work. As someone who spends her life in the world of storytelling and helping leaders navigate complexity, I found myself thinking, 'I wish I had this in my hands sooner.' It's a smart, human guide for anyone trying to lead with authenticity and heart in complicated times."*

—Lindsay Shookus
Seven-Time Emmy Winning Producer,
Leadership Coach, and Speaker

"This book deftly weaves together themes from research and lived experience as a leader and advisor to illuminate how well-meaning leaders get badly off track—and what they can do instead. Dr. Monahan illustrates her insights with compelling, resonant storytelling to help make abstract principles crystallize for the reader. Timely and relevant, this is a genuinely exceptional leadership book!"

—Alexis Fink
Former VP, People Analytics and Workforce Strategy, Meta,
Senior Research Scientist, Center for Effective Organizations

"Through the power of storytelling, Reclaim the Plot *reminds us that for humans, the stories we tell each other are the reality we often create. In the book, Kelly delivers a powerful set of stories grounded in scenarios everyone can identify with, using science to illustrate how unintended consequences can result from not digging into second and third-order effects. This is a must-read for leaders and aspiring leaders for how to navigate through tough decisions by keeping longer-term outcomes in mind and using the power of stories to shape narratives."*

—Kyle Forrest
Future of HR Leader, Deloitte Consulting LLP

"I've lived the Driftwell story. I know what it costs to chase performance at the expense of people, and I know what it takes to find your way back. In the age of AI, the most dangerous leadership question isn't 'how do we move faster?'—it's 'what are we leaving behind?' Dr. Kelly Monahan puts that question at the center of a story so real it demands your attention. This book won't let you look away. Are you moving fast, or moving right?"

—Jen Fisher
Bestselling Author of *Hope Is the Strategy*

"Work has changed. Most leadership playbooks have not. In Reclaim the Plot, *Kelly Monahan makes a compelling case for why organizations need to stop performing outdated models of work and start building ones that are more honest, adaptive, and human."*

—Brian Elliott
CEO, Work Forward

"I read Reclaim the Plot *and kept thinking: I need this book. EVERY leader needs this book. Kelly Monahan shows us, scene by scene, what it costs when we choose speed over humanity and what it takes to find our way back. Honest, deeply human, and urgently needed."*

—Lisa Sun
Gravitas CEO and Bestselling Author of *Gravitas*

"Reclaim the Plot *is a compelling and refreshingly human look at leadership in an era defined by technological disruption, complexity, and constant uncertainty. By blending research with storytelling, Monahan masterfully captures the quiet, high-stakes decisions leaders face every day—and why rethinking how we work has never been more urgent."*

—Dan Schawbel
Bestselling Author of *Back to Human*

"Many books will tell you how and why business today is broken. But only one, Kelly Monahan's Reclaim the Plot, *blends a creative exploration of fictional company Driftwell with real-world data and insights gleaned from Monahan's two decades as a behavioral researcher and corporate executive. This is a must read for those aspiring to lead with human integrity in and through the age of AI."*

—Alexandra Levit
Workforce Futurist and Author of *Deep Talent* and *Make School Work*

"Kelly has written the book every executive needs right now. Rigorous research, radical honesty, and a story so recognizable it will make you catch your breath. I have always said that leaders set the standards of everything, and this book proves exactly why that standard must start with people. People have always been, and will always be, the most important asset in any business. Profits follow purpose. Results follow relationships. And sustainable success is built with humans at the center. If you care about the people you lead, and you want to build something that lasts, read this book, it's exceptional."

—Neen James
Client Experience Expert and Author of *Exceptional Experiences*

Reclaim *the* Plot

HOW LEADERS REWRITE THE STORY WHEN AI REWRITES WORK

KELLY MONAHAN
NATIONAL BESTSELLING AUTHOR OF *ESSENTIAL*

WILEY

Published by John Wiley & Sons, Inc., Hoboken, New Jersey.

Library of Congress Cataloging-in-Publication Data is Available:

ISBN 9781394426171 (Cloth)
ISBN 9781394426188 (ePub)
ISBN 9781394426195 (ePDF)

Cover Design and Image: Wiley
Author Photo: Courtesy of Kelly Monahan

Printed and bound by CPI Group (UK) Ltd, Croydon, CR0 4YY

C9781394426171_030826

For Lincoln and Dean, may we find
the courage to reclaim the plot and restore
hope to the workplace your generation will one day inherit.

Contents

Introduction: Why the Future of Leadership Speaks in Stories, Not Data

The future of leadership will be written in stories, not dashboards.

Leaders today are trying to absorb more information than ever before. Even as a researcher, I'm overwhelmed by the sheer volume of studies released each day. One of my favorite databases, arXiv, now publishes nearly 700 new academic papers daily. No human mind can absorb knowledge at that speed.

What I've discovered over the past year is that business leaders don't need another data point. We already have more than we can process. Every system we've built to measure progress is flashing red. Economies are faltering, motivation is waning, and institutions are buckling under their own contradictions. The problem isn't a lack of information; it's a lack of courage and conviction in our shared humanity.[1] And that's leaving many leaders feeling exhausted, stuck, and alone. And if I'm being honest, I've begun to question whether the battle scars of my own corporate leadership were worth the cost.

For the past twenty years, I've had a front-row seat in the modern workplace, working alongside executives at some of the most fascinating companies in the world. As a researcher focused on the future of work, I've been invited into C-suites where few outsiders get to sit. And nearly every leader I've met carries the same private fear: *What if I'm left behind in the future of work?*

I grew up in Rochester, New York, so I understand that fear. No one wants to be the next Kodak, which was once a symbol of innovation but is now a cautionary tale. No one wants to be remembered as the leader who missed the next digital revolution. Rather, leaders want to go out on top, reinventing the old while ushering in the new.

And as a trained researcher, I can't help but observe these critical leadership moments as if I'm in the experimental phase of a research study. While watching leadership teams scramble in the wake of digital disruption, I noticed a pattern in human behavior that led me to conclude that the future of work has never been just about the technology change. It is also acutely about what happens to people when their systems start to crack, when organizations move faster than the people inside them can keep up. This is when disruption stops being a moment and becomes a way of life.

I've watched leaders chase every new tool and data-backed transformation plan, believing that progress alone would save them from the wave about to crash at their doorstep. Yet, beneath the dashboards and quarterly results, something essential starts to slip away: the shared human experience that makes work worth doing.

Humanity came to the forefront during the pandemic and then quickly swung into the background as soon as signs of a new normal emerged. This is why Christie Smith and I were compelled to write *Essential*. We recognized early on that bringing the human spirit back into leadership decision-making is a performance unlock and that it requires leaders to put the heart of their organizations first. We joined forces to provide the science, data, and credible research to get the attention of today's leaders.

We combined our years of leadership experience with the proven research to help leaders stay on track.

As a keynote speaker with a new book, I set out to offer the highest level of validity, evidence, and outcomes I could. It was on these speaking circuits that I came across a dangerous and compelling leadership distraction—new voices filling the space of the unknown via expensive retreats with the promise of enlightenment-for-the-elite. Well-meaning individuals convince leaders that being human at work is a mystery only a few can decode, and for the right price tag, the secrets of humanity can be theirs. I recently attended one of these experiences and lived to tell the tale.

I was invited to speak at a company that was bringing together its top leadership teams for a year-end meeting. This group was still reeling from a deep workforce reduction that left many wondering how the work would even get done in the new year. Being a researcher and having spent years studying how to lead through disruption, I knew what the workforce needed at that moment. They needed leaders to provide clarity, alignment, and space to acknowledge the grief that had been sitting beneath the surface. The layoffs had occurred less than two months before this gathering and were still fresh, raw, and haunting. I was honored to have the opportunity to help this group navigate this challenging time. Unfortunately, I didn't get to speak first.

Instead, the CEO kicked off by saying it was time to move on, no more talk about the layoffs. The leadership team was done being sad, and there was work to get done. They were here to move on. Then they proceeded to hand the mic to the other keynote speaker, who identified as a "CEO Whisperer" with long hair and crystals around his neck. He has never worked a day in corporate in his life, yet he has the secrets to unite this room.

He began telling stories of his LSD trips and how spending five nights underground with no light or human contact was the key to finding his own sense of humanity. He then shared, with striking candor, the childhood trauma he experienced from his mother and how it led him to a profound conclusion: that love is the answer to everything. The CEO Whisperer concluded the session by blasting electronic dance music into the room, asking the audience to beat their chests, literally, just like the scene from *The Wolf of Wall Street*, and ended with directing the executive team to snort loudly for three minutes to rediscover their own sense of shared belonging.

As I sat in the front row of the audience with my jaw on the ground, he finally ended his musings with a simple solution: We just needed more love in business. You know that feeling when someone says the right words in all the wrong ways? To say it bluntly, it was cringe.

Talk about losing the plot.

I attempted to bring the room back to center when it was time for my keynote. However, many leaders had left after that session, needing some fresh air, while others started reading the chapter on LSD and creativity that was in front of them. Needless to say, attention was everywhere but on the stage. I left that experience thinking about how far we've drifted from what humanity in leadership means. It isn't about performative vulnerability or orchestrated healing experiences.

It's about the nuanced work of rebuilding trust after loss.

It's the courage to acknowledge pain and grief instead of rushing past it.

It's choosing clarity over theatrics, empathy over performance.

Leadership doesn't need to be sensationalized to be human. It just needs to be remembered.

That day stays with me. Not just because of the absurdity of the moment, but because it revealed how lost we've become in our search for meaning at work, especially at the very top. We choose to outsource the wisdom of our deeper selves to consultants, workshops, and wellness gurus. But wisdom in leadership is the one thing that can't be outsourced.

Choosing to be human at work is built into our daily choices. It's in how leaders speak when the room is heavy, how they make sense of loss, how they hold people steady in the unknown. The human spirit is deep within each of us, mirroring and reflecting who we all really are back to one another.

But, somewhere along the way, business traded integrity and meaning for market performance. We started rewarding charisma over character, efficiency over connection. Leadership was never meant to be sterile or detached. It was meant to be deeply human. So that's where this cautionary tale begins, how one well-meaning leadership team lost its way, and what it will take to find it again.

At the exact moment leaders most need clarity about what makes us human, artificial intelligence (AI) has stepped onto the main stage. Of course, AI isn't new. It's been plainly waiting in the wings since the 1950s. But now, it has entered our daily lives with a force that's shaken every business and every leader I know. Like the dot-com era, it arrived wrapped in promise. Headlines warn that AI is going to change everything about work, value, and leadership itself.

But this "once-in-a-lifetime" moment comes with a crushing weight. I've felt it myself. The relentless demand for speed and scale, often at the expense of what makes us human. Leadership has never been harder. It's also never been less envied. Research from LinkedIn shows that only 30% of today's workforce aspires to lead.[2] The weight of decisions, the constant pressure to anticipate every turn, the expectation to do what once took three people. It's no wonder leadership has lost its luster.

So, I'm writing this book as a *cautionary tale*.

Because I've noticed a pattern from leaders who are getting this right today.

The ones who thrive in these upside-down conditions share a common thread: they've learned to balance humanity and technology. They understand data and systems, but they also understand hearts. Their pursuit of innovation is matched by their pursuit of meaning. They haven't lost the plot of what business is really about.

I wish I could say the same for myself.

Somewhere along the way, I got caught up in the chase running toward the next promotion, the next paycheck, the next big AI breakthrough. I appeared on national television to discuss AI's impact and wrote countless articles advising others on how to lead in this new world. But when I finally looked in the mirror, I realized my own human spirit was dimming.

I had an early fear, after I completed my graduate studies, that I hadn't led enough to teach leadership, so I plunged headfirst into corporate America. However, this fear had evolved into something darker. I, too, had lost my way. I began chasing numbers over people. I started to believe that business couldn't be about both people *and* profits, that I had to choose. And the choice to prioritize profits felt, at the time, like the only way to survive.

As W. Edwards Deming warned, *"A bad system will beat a good person every time."*[3] I watched that truth unfold around me, and within me. That's why this book is different.

My earlier work focused on the science of management and behavioral economics, which was intellectually rigorous but emotionally safe. My second book made the business case for a people-first approach to business, but even then, I hid behind research and case studies that weren't mine.

This time, I'm writing without a corporate filter or PR polish. I'm weaving decades of research with the lived reality, and the scars, of leading in today's workplace. I've turned to storytelling and poetry because, when systems collapse, it's often the poets and storytellers who help us find meaning again. Story and verse name the emotions we're not yet brave enough to say out loud.

I've also taken Brené Brown's challenge to heart: to lead courageously. So, rather than relying on someone else's examples, I'm drawing from my own. Over the past twenty years, I've worked within some of the most fascinating organizations across finance, consulting, and technology. Certain leadership patterns transcend industry and I've distilled those into a single fictional company: Driftwell.

Through Driftwell, you'll meet leaders who embody the habits, blind spots, and contradictions I've observed for years. They are not villains. Most began with good intentions, only to drift and lose their way. Their stories are cautionary tales of what happens when purpose fades and performance becomes the only currency.

Throughout the book, you'll move between Driftwell's story, research-backed commentary, hot takes, reflective exercises, and Coaching Corners. Each part is designed to help you see the same leadership pattern from a different angle: first through the story, then through the evidence, and finally through your own reflection.

You'll also hear from I/O psychologist and executive coach Kim Fazio in the Coaching Corners. Kim is an ICF-certified coach who advises Fortune 500 executive leaders and has been a trusted coach and thinking partner to me for years. Her perspective helps translate the Driftwell story into practical reflection for leaders. Where the narrative shows how leaders drift, Kim's Coaching Corners offer a grounded pause to help readers notice their own patterns, ask better questions, and find a way back to clarity, courage, and shared humanity at work.

I share these stories not to blame, but to illuminate what's shared, which is the very human experience of trying to lead while the world tilts beneath us. The names and companies are fictionalized, but the feelings are not. These are the moments we've all lived in some form. The exhaustion, the cynicism, the wondering of *whether the system is too broken to be human*.

As a behavioral researcher, I know this much: no one starts out wanting to burn people out, strip meaning from work, or automate livelihoods out of existence. Not one early leadership conversation begins that way. But many end there.

So, I invite you to read these stories as mirrors; a safe place to reflect on your own leadership journey. Pay attention to what moves you, what stirs discomfort, what language resonates. Let the stories remind you that leadership isn't a title; it's a reflection of our shared humanity at work.

And if there's still a part of you that longs to lead with more balance, to bring heart back into the work without losing the edge of performance, then this book is for you. You'll learn about AI along the way, but more importantly, you'll rediscover what it means to be human in the age of the algorithm.

Through the rise and fall of Driftwell and the research that follows, I invite you to return not to some idealized past, but to the humanity that's already within you. Your people, your organizations, and those who will lead after you are counting on it.

Prelude: The Urgent Meeting

Date: August 5, 2025

The city was still half-asleep, but on the thirty-fourth floor of Driftwell's headquarters, the day already felt spent.

The boardroom glowed an anxious blue from the wall of screens that broadcast dashboards, headlines, the live ticker pulsing red: DRFT –18.7% ↓. Surrounded by all the modern technology, it sometimes felt less like a business meeting and more like a war room. Cold light pooled over the executives' faces, pale and unnatural. Someone's phone buzzed and went silent.

Jim Cramer gestured wildly on mute. Even without sound, everyone knew the rhythm of his outrage.

On the main display, a CNBC headline screamed across the top:

> **PRIVATE EQUITY FIRM BLASTS DRIFTWELL LEADERSHIP FOR LOSING FOCUS ON CORE CUSTOMERS. THREATENS CEO REMOVAL.**

Coffee cups lined the table, untouched. The pastries in the center had begun to harden in the chill of the air-conditioning. The only movement was the steady flicker of the ticker and the faint hum of the projector. It was a mechanical heartbeat in a room that had forgotten how to breathe.

The meeting hadn't been scheduled. It appeared after midnight, dropped onto calendars by assistants who never left the building, the subject line a single word: "Urgent."

By the time the first executives arrived, the air already carried the weight of something unspoken. They hesitated before sitting, gauging distance from the head of the table as though proximity might offer protection.

Then Anna walked in. Driftwell's CEO. Once described by *Fortune* as "the heartbeat of biotech." This morning, she looked like someone running on borrowed adrenaline. Her posture was upright, but her eyes were tired in a way makeup couldn't disguise.

She opened her laptop. The hinge squeaked, breaking the hush. She didn't even start with a hello.

"They've lost sight of their core customers," she read aloud, "failing to manage costs or innovation effectively." Her voice was low and flat. Each word dragging through exhaustion.

She slammed the laptop shut. The sound cracked through the silence like a gavel.

Graham, the CFO, didn't look up. His reflection hovered in the screen, jaw set. "They're not wrong," he said quietly. "Revenue's down nine percent. Retention's slipping. The Street thinks we've gone chasing trends that won't pay off." He glanced at Priya who he blamed for putting Driftwell in position.

The ticker jumped again: DRFT –21.3% ↓.

Across the table, Priya, the young CTO, leaned back, the calmest person in the room. Her smartwatch glowed red, tracking her heart rate. "Or maybe they're too shortsighted to see what we're building," she said. "Our AI platform *is* the future. These investors just can't see it yet."

Anna's head turned sharply. "We've invested eighty million dollars, Priya. And I still can't clearly explain what we're building."

Priya took a slow breath, unbothered. "Maybe we just need to reset the energy in this room. A quick meditation—"

James, the CHRO, cut her off. "People are burning out, Priya. They're not robots, though you treat them as such." His voice carried the weary steadiness of someone who'd been holding a truth too long.

Anna's jaw tightened. "We said we'd act like founders. Founders push through when it's hard. 996[1] is the new Valley standard. We can't ease up now."

"Founders also have ownership," James replied. "You froze equity last year. You can't take away the upside and still demand devotion."

The projector hummed louder, as if leaning in.

"The board meets Monday," Graham said finally. "If we don't show discipline, they'll find someone who will. We need to cut costs."

Anna's voice thinned. "How deep?"

"Twenty-five percent. That gets us to positive cash flow in two quarters."

Anna blinked. "That's a thousand jobs, Graham."

Priya raised her cup of cold coffee, her bracelets chiming softly. "We call them skill-based roles now, not jobs. AI can take on most of it. This isn't really a loss, it's evolution. It's all in how we frame it."

James turned to her, incredulous. "You're evolving past your conscience."

"Enough," Anna said, voice raising as she slammed her palm against the table. "Frame it as a strategic reset externally. We'll say we're returning to our roots and it's all about staying focused, disciplined, customer-first. We will directly address this PE firm in the daylight."

Graham nodded, already typing. "I'll have projections tonight."

Priya smiled faintly. "And I'll align the AI roadmap to customer outcomes. It'll look deliberate."

James leaned back, rubbing his temples. "What do I tell the people who built this company? They'll see through this in a second."

Anna stared out the window, the skyline sharpening in the morning light. "Tell them this is how Driftwell survives. Thank them. Draft tight NDAs. I don't want a mess on our hands."

The ticker flickered again: DRFT –27.4% ↓.

Anna gathered her notes. "I want the plan in twenty-four hours."

They rose in silence. Priya gave Anna a quick pat on the shoulder, more of a forced gesture than felt solidarity. Graham straightened his tie, looking relieved that there was a plan to recover the balance sheets that had been red for three straight quarters.

James stayed seated, eyes on the Driftwell logo pulsing on the wall. It was a stylized wave, breaking and reforming in an endless loop. It had once meant innovation. Now it looked like a warning.

He watched it shimmer a moment longer and thought: *Driftwell.* Funny how drift looks a lot like freefall today. Outside, the city began its day. Inside, the machines kept humming, while a thousand futures quietly began to end.

ACT I

The Drift

Where leadership begins to lose its humanity.

It doesn't happen overnight but begins in moments like the one you just witnessed. The unraveling is marked by a discrete, logical, bottom-line-oriented mindset. A spreadsheet replaces a conversation. A metric replaces a name. Someone says, "*We're doing what we must.*" And everyone nods, because that's what survival sounds like in a boardroom.

But the drift starts long before the layoff. It begins twenty years earlier, in the places that shaped the people now sitting at that table. It begins in the classrooms, the case studies, the polished ambitions that taught them how to lead and, unknowingly, how to lose touch with the human side of business.

What follows isn't a traditional business book. It's a cautionary tale told through the rise and unraveling of Driftwell and its leaders.

Within this first act, you'll move through four scenes that trace that drift:

- **Scene 1: The drift from trust.** Inside the eMBA classroom where modern leadership's subtle cynicism first takes root.
- **Scene 2: The drift toward profits.** When the AI gold rush blinds leaders to purpose and value.
- **Scene 3: The drift from a shared reality.** When "startup mode" becomes a story leaders tell themselves, and no one else believes.
- **Scene 4: The drift to delirium.** When the layoff arrives, and detachment masquerades as discipline.

Each scene is fictionalized, but every one is true, drawn from decades of research and lived experience. Driftwell isn't one company; it's the story of what happens when a business forgets it's made of people.

Read these stories not as fiction, but as reflection. You may recognize your own meeting rooms, your own language, even your own blind spots. *The Drift* isn't just what happens to companies. It's what happens to us when we forget that leadership was never about control or valuation. It was, and still is, about staying human while the world accelerates around us.

To understand how these leaders ended up at that table, exhausted and divided, we have to go back twenty years and step into a classroom where this outcome always felt inevitable.

Scene 1: The Theory of Everyone Else

Anna's Beginning: January 25, 2005

The lecture hall buzzed with loud ambition. Keyboards clicked as people frenetically answered emails, espresso hissed in the hallway after another long night of work, and the introductions were so overinflated that they reeked of corner office ambition.

Anna slipped into the front row and set her bag beside her chair. The scrape of metal legs dragging against the tile sounded deliberate. A small declaration that she intended to own this room.

The business school gleamed like a shrine to success: floor-to-ceiling glass, brushed steel, and corporate sponsor logos etched into every surface. It looked less like a classroom than a trading floor for future power.

Above the chalkboard hung a plaque in bold silver type:

"Only the paranoid survive."

—Andy Grove, CEO, Intel

Anna smiled. *Finally*, she thought. A commandment I can live by.

She scanned the room. Polished suits, confident smiles, everyone ready for the C-suite. *Which one will I be competing with for a* Fortune *cover?* she wondered. The imaginary headline flashed in her mind: ***The Biotech Visionary Who Saved Lives and Markets.***

She was still lost in that thought when someone tapped her shoulder.

"Hi, I'm Graham."

He had the kind of handshake that belonged in investor meetings. It was direct, unflinching. *A competitor*, she decided.

"Anna," she replied. "So, what's the endgame?"

"CFO," he said without hesitation. "Fast-growth tech. Something cool."

He radiated a dangerous confidence.

"And you?" he asked.

"I want to build something," she said. "My own company, maybe biotech. Doing good *and* doing well."

"Then remember me when you make it," he grinned. "Every CEO needs a CFO."

They both laughed, the way students laugh with optimism before the future hardens into reality.

The professor finally arrived, wrestling with the projector cable until a student stepped in to help. The screen blinked to life as a slide appeared with a single word in bold: **Leadership.**

He didn't bother with small talk. "You're here because you're different," he began. "Ambitious. Competitive. Wired for the C-suite."

Anna straightened in her chair.

"Let's start with agency theory," he continued, advancing the slide. "People are self-interested. Your job as leaders is to put in measures that control that self-interest and compel people to act on behalf of shareholders or investors."

A few students chuckled. Anna didn't. The word *control* hung in the air like static. It unsettled her but also thrilled her a little too. Control meant certainty. Certainty meant power.

The professor paced as he pontificated. "Most people don't actually want to work. Given the choice, they'll act in their own self-interest. That's why leadership exists: to ensure employees act in shareholders' interests. Incentives. Accountability. Guardrails. Carrots and sticks."

Heads nodded. Anna's pen raced across her notebook.

He clicked again: **Businesses are not people, and therefore not moral.**

"The most moral thing a company can do," he said, "is maximize profit."

A hand shot up from the back. "But wasn't that the thinking that led to Enron?"

The professor's expression thinned. "Ethics matter, of course. But regulation matters more. We can't rely on people to do the right thing; we have to make them."

Beside her, Graham whispered, "Sarbanes–Oxley, my daily nightmare."

The professor caught it. "Care to enlighten us, Mr. . . .?"

"Graham," he said, standing easily. "SOX established corporate accountability after Enron. Internal controls. Audit integrity. The paperwork never ends."

A few students laughed. The professor looked grudgingly impressed.

Anna watched him, intrigued. Even under pressure, he looked composed, almost smug. *He'll make CFO someday*, she thought. *The question is whether I'll make it all the way to the top.*

The lecture is winding down. Rows of laptops swiftly shut in practiced rhythm like the sound of ambition packing up for the day.

The professor erases the final equation: **Oversight = Performance.** The words smear into a gray haze, chalk dust catching the light like smoke.

Anna lingers; pen still poised over her notebook. On the page, she's circled one phrase three times: *People must be managed.* Around it, she's drawn arrows, formulas, and margin notes, trying to make the concept fit inside her sense of rightness.

Through the glass wall, she can see the campus lawn outside, sunlight scattered across students sprawled on the grass. It's loud with laughter, movement, and possibility. It's the world she'll soon be asked to organize, optimize, and measure.

Graham taps her shoulder on his way out.

"Coming?" he asks.

"In a minute."

She waits until the room empties. She looks again at the quote above the chalkboard, glowing faintly in the afternoon light: *Only the paranoid survive.*

For a fleeting second, she feels the weight of it, as if the words are less advice and more prophecy. Then she closes her notebook with certainty, tucks it under her arm, and walks out, heels echoing against the tile.

On the desk behind her, a single page is left behind. It's the syllabus for next week's class:

Week 2—Incentive Design and Performance Metrics.

The door clicks shut. Next week, they'll learn how to design performance systems that keep people aligned with the interests of the organization, where incentives guide behavior and deviations are quickly corrected.

Commentary: What We Teach, We Become

This is how the drift begins, not with malevolence, but with lesson plans, not with greed, but with grades.

In classrooms like Anna's, business theory hardened into belief. What was once a field about people became a science of scalability. By the time the case studies reached the front of the room, leadership wasn't a human practice anymore; it was a control system.

When I first began lecturing in these same kinds of classrooms, I noticed it too—the hierarchy between head and heart. Students wanted certainty, not nuance. They wanted a playbook that promised success, not a conversation that questioned what success should mean. You could almost feel their shoulders relax when I said "data." But mention "trust," and half the room shifted in their seats.

It wasn't always this way. A century ago, management theorist and social worker, Mary Parker Follett, wrote about the "law of the situation," which held that leadership isn't about power over others, but power *with* them. She advocated that no one person should have constant power, but that the situation should dictate who is best positioned to make a decision. She saw organizations as living systems of collaboration, where the leader's role was to integrate human energy toward a common purpose. Long before "systems thinking" or "psychological safety" became buzzwords, Follett argued that management should be rooted in relationships, not control.

And yet, somewhere along the line, her voice faded. By the time I entered the workforce in the early 2000s, business school halls had replaced her relational wisdom with something far shinier: the language of VUCA, which stands for volatility, uncertainty, complexity, and ambiguity. It was the acronym of my early career, the water every young leader swam in. We were taught to brace for turbulence, to plan for chaos, to survive disruption. What no one told us was how that constant vigilance would change us.

When you live inside a VUCA world long enough, you start leading as if people are threats to be managed rather than allies to be trusted. The systems we built for control became a form of armor, a protection against risk, and eventually, against one another. That's when humanity began to leak out of the system.

We built organizations that reward intellect over empathy, precision over perception. Somewhere between spreadsheets and shareholder reports, the purpose of business, which was once framed as service to others, was reframed as something purely mechanical: maximize output, minimize friction.

The results are visible everywhere. Organizations designed for control inevitably produce exhaustion. Systems built on distrust demand endless oversight. The more we try to measure people, the less we seem to understand them.

Leaders like Anna and Graham graduate fluent in finance and strategy, but nearly illiterate in the psychology of trust. They enter the workforce believing that control is leadership and every incentive system, performance review, and "leadership competency model" reinforces that belief.

Here's the paradox: what we teach about human nature eventually becomes self-fulfilling. Teach leaders that people are lazy, and they'll build systems that prove it. Teach leaders that people are capable, and they'll build systems that unleash it.

The stories we tell about human behavior don't just describe reality; they *create* it.

When I ask Executive MBAs in classrooms today whether they believe most people want to work, the answers are rarely surprising. There's a pause, then someone admits: "Honestly? No. Most people do the bare minimum."

Then I follow up with, "Do *you* want to work?" Every hand rises. Every time.

That's the moment drift becomes visible. It's immediately seen in the split between how leaders see themselves and how they see everyone else.

Research calls it the *fundamental attribution error*. I just call it losing the plot. *Because once you stop believing people want to do good work, you start building systems that ensure they can't.* We've taught generations of leaders to assume humans are self-interested, and then watched as they designed organizations that proved themselves right.

The Research: Can We Trust People to Work?

What follows isn't theory. It's the story of how trust softly leaked out of the workplace.

It started, as most things do, with good intentions and bad assumptions. In the early 1900s, mechanical engineer Frederick Taylor declared that "hardly a competent workman can be found who does not study how slowly he can work and still convince his employer he's going at a good pace."[1] That single line became the blueprint for modern management. A century later, we're still living inside it.

Taylor turned leadership into math. He believed people couldn't be trusted, so he built systems to measure, monitor, and motivate them. Over time, those systems hardened into gospel, which are taught in business schools, reinforced by politics, and mocked in movies like *Office Space*. What began as a humanities discipline became an engineering problem: how to make humans more efficient.

Ironically, the more we measure people, the less we seem to trust them. Behavioral economics later gave this phenomenon a name. What we believe about human nature shapes how we design organizations, and those designs in turn shape how people behave.

- When we teach leaders that individuals are lazy or self-interested, they build systems to control them.
- When we teach leaders cooperation and interdependence, they build systems to help them flourish.

One experiment still stuns me. Researchers handed students a stack of 250 tokens.[2] They could keep them in a personal account for a guaranteed return or invest them in a shared pool that would multiply and be divided evenly. In theory, if everyone contributed, everyone would win. But if anyone held back, they'd profit from everyone else's generosity.

The twist? Economics students who'd spent years studying self-interest kept nearly 80% for themselves. Conversely, nursing students, steeped in care and empathy, gave away almost half. Same math, different mindset.

When asked why, the economics students didn't hesitate: "That's just rational." Fairness barely registered. It wasn't that they were colder people. They were simply acting out the story they'd been taught.

Another classic experiment used the *ultimatum game*: two people split a sum of money.[3] Offer too little, and your partner can reject it—leaving you both with nothing. In most groups, people offer about half. Economics majors offered fewer dollars and accepted more unfair offers. They'd learned that self-interest was rational and cooperation optional.

My favorite version of this came later, when researchers renamed the same activity. Half the group played "The Wall Street Game." The other half played "The Community Game." Same rules, same payoff. Only the label changed. Those playing "Wall Street" competed twice as often. Those playing "Community" cooperated.[4]

Nothing else mattered, including education, IQ, or personality. Just the story they thought they were in. When we call business a *war*, people start looking for enemies. When we call it a *community*, they start looking for each other. The metaphors we use become moral instructions.

As sociologist C. Wright Mills once put it, "*We influence a man by naming his acts or imputing motives to them.*"[5] When we tell people that the world runs on self-interest, they begin to act as though it does. And soon, that story becomes reality. And for many people today, that reality has created a lived experience that simply doesn't work.

Hot Take: When a Lack of Trust Moves Outside the Classroom

To be fair, the context around leadership has shifted dramatically. Precariousness has become the norm, unsettling every layer of business. Macroeconomic models are no longer effective as tariffs fluctuate and inflation rises. The polarization of both employees and customers has compelled brands to adopt political identities they never intended to take on. And technology, instead of simplifying, often multiplies the complexity. All of this has made the work of managing and developing talent harder than ever before, further straining the belief that people do indeed want to work today.

When I joined Meta as its first Future of Work Research Lead, it felt like one of the coolest jobs imaginable. We were still deep in the pandemic, and remote work was a brand-new muscle for the company. It may sound surprising that the same industry building the tools for virtual collaboration often resists using them to rethink work, but it's true. Some of the most technologically advanced companies I've worked with have the most traditional people practices.

While I was running experiments in virtual reality to figure out how to host meetings in the metaverse, I was also leading studies to understand how remote work was actually working. Despite the rhetoric of innovation, there was a deeply held belief that "real" work could only happen in person. As the workforce became more distributed, the question "How do we get people back to the office?" became existential.

For a year, I ran analysis after analysis with a team of brilliant PhD data scientists to uncover what worked. We found that the traditional "moments that matter" in HR needed a serious refresh. Onboarding thrived when it began face-to-face. Project kickoffs benefited from an initial in-person gathering. Big wins deserve to be celebrated together. But between those milestones, people worked just as effectively, albeit often better, on their own terms.

The problem was that there was no playbook for this work rhythm. It required a deep level of trust within teams and comfort with ambiguity at the top. It required discretion and a willingness to admit that one size doesn't fit all. It required leaders to treat people like adults capable of making adult decisions. Trusting people ultimately meant sharing leadership power.

That was a risk few were willing to take. And so, like many others, the company returned to the office, which meant returning to the comfort of control and distancing itself from the possibility of something new. The old playbook reigned, while a new one sat behind scattered Google Docs and meeting notes, never to be written.

It was another moment where I experienced how organizations drift, not because of the technology but because of the struggle to trust each other.

> **For all our talk about innovation, we still lead with fear—a deep fear of losing control, of being left behind, of trusting people too much. We chase the future through technology while clinging to the past in how we manage people.**

And until leaders can acknowledge those contradictions honestly, we'll continue to mistake progress for advancement.

Reflective Exercise: The Beliefs Beneath Your Behavior

I now turn to you. What do you think? Do most people want to do the right thing at work? Can people be trusted? Your answer changes everything about the way you approach your job and the way you lead today. If you went through a similar MBA program to Anna's, then the answer might be no. Or your own lived experience may confirm your assumption that most people are unreliable and disengaged.

One of my favorite thinkers in this space is writer and management consultant, Dr. Meg Wheatley, who offers an alternative perspective on how to think about people at work. She describes sane leadership as "the unwavering belief that people can be generous, creative, and kind. It is a place where the best human qualities can manifest even in the midst of fear and turmoil. . . leaders choose to use their power and influence to support the human spirit rather than control it."[6]

Table I.1 illustrates how we present ourselves and design work, depending on the assumptions we hold. Please look at the work design elements and reflect on which column most accurately describes your world of work today. To aid with the reflection, consider the following prompts before moving on to the next scene in Driftwell's story.

Table I.1 How our assumptions shape the world of work

Work design element	Assumption 1: People don't want to work	Assumption 2: People do want to work
Core belief	People are naturally lazy and must be controlled or motivated.	People are naturally curious and want to contribute meaningfully.
Leadership style	Command and control: monitor, measure, correct.	Trust and enable: coach, connect, and remove barriers.
Organizational structure	Hierarchical, compliance-driven, focused on oversight.	Networked, purpose-driven, focused on autonomy and collaboration.
Motivation system	External rewards and punishments (bonuses, threats, key performance indicators).	Intrinsic motivation (purpose, mastery, belonging).
Workplace culture	Fear-based: "Don't mess up."	Growth-based: "Learn and adapt."
Performance measurement	Hours logged, visible effort, short-term outputs.	Value created, learning, long-term outcomes.
Role of manager	Enforcer of discipline.	Builder of context and clarity.
View of humanity	People must be fixed or optimized.	People are capable and evolving.
Impact on innovation	Conformity and risk aversion.	Experimentation and creativity.
Emotional climate	Cynicism and burnout.	Energy and shared ownership.

Rewriting the Plot of Work

1. Think of a moment when you felt *most alive* at work. What assumption about human nature was operating in that environment? Did you trust others around you to bring their best selves to work?
2. Now think of a time when you felt *most drained* at work. What assumption seemed to be driving leadership behavior at that time? Was a lack of trust a contributing factor? Were you playing more politics than doing the work itself?
3. Write one sentence that begins: "If I truly believed people want to work, I would lead differently by. . ."

Scene 2: Blinded by the Stock

August 10, 2023 (approximately two years before the opening boardroom scene)

Anonymous Reddit post on r/driftwell

You showed me your graph.
It rose, up and up, like a prayer to the market gods.
You mistook my silence for awe.

It could double again.
My bank account stayed still,
but your pupils dilated with profit.

The stock price blinded you,
never seeing the talent bleeding below.

You asked for weekends,
for faster, for more shine,
until the glow became the glare.

Your MBA taught you trickle-down economics.
But the tide never came.

The trickle was too slow.
The rich floated; the rest of us drowned.

There's only one way out:
stand up,
walk out.
Let the crash happen without me underneath it.

#Anna #Graham

Comments

+1. All they care about is the money.

Has anyone else seen the insane compensation packages for Driftwell's leaders?! And for what?

Couldn't have said it better myself. Been here for a few years and seen the place go downhill. It used to be about the people, but the top people seem to care only about profits.

I hope the Driftwell leaders see this. Their greed is running this place into the ground.

What happened to the medicine here? I get we are a public company, but are we even doing good anymore?

The post spread like wildfire through Driftwell before lunch. Phone screens glowed, Slack threads buzzed, and even the interns were whispering.

Anna's heels characteristically struck the polished tile as she walked briskly toward her office, the sound sharp against the dull hum of the open workspace. Graham's voice cut through behind her—"Anna! Wait up—"

She didn't. Not yet. The company she built was bleeding credibility in real time. And the worst part? She couldn't tell if the post was wrong.

"Anna, we really need to talk." Graham was nearly out of breath trying to catch up to Anna. A few brave workers turned from their screens to watch the executives scrambling down the hall.

Sensing the stares, Anna lowered her voice to a strained whisper. "Graham, we have to put out this fire. I can't have our internal teams turning on us. We are so close to a product breakthrough here. I need them laser-focused on building, not shitposting to this stupid thread."

James, the company's CHRO, was already in her office multitasking on his laptop as he waited for Anna to arrive. He had a mixture of anxiety and annoyance regarding the anonymous posting that was going to derail his day. And each time he refreshed his feed, the comments kept piling up, echoing the bleak sentiments of the voice before.

Anna took a seat behind her desk and invited Graham to sit next to James on the other side. Anna opened her energy drink, but the caffeine wasn't cutting through the fatigue anymore. James's laptop pinged again. It was another notification of a new comment on the thread. She flinched at the sound.

"Okay, James, have you been able to identify this poster yet? Do we think it's someone currently employed here or a disgruntled person we let go?" Anna's dark brown eyes remained on James, seeking to assess his sense of urgency on this.

"Anna, I've reached out to Reddit, but it's against their policy to share any sort of identifying information. I even just asked for an IP location to see if we could do some triangulation, but they aren't budging."

"Well, how do we get this to stop? The comments are too much. I know it's not personal, but even I am having trouble getting through some of them. And if I'm getting distracted by this, then you both know all those people out there are too."

"I understand. Let me get a pulse survey out, and let's hold a town hall next week. Let's reinforce our commitment to our people, and honestly, just getting some face time with you, Anna, will go a long way."

"Graham, you're quiet. What do you think?"

"Anna, I don't want to be rude, but I don't really care about the posting. I am here to talk about a potential acquisition that is urgent." Graham shifted his eyes toward James to wrap this up so he could get back to business.

Anna looked back at James, the strain from not sleeping clearly visible in her eyes. "James, schedule the town hall and get that pulse survey out. And please script my portion for next week. I don't have time for this, and you need to make this as light a lift as possible for me."

James let out a sigh. He was used to playing the cleanup role since joining Driftwell. He knew Anna was a sharp business leader and could even be considered ruthless when necessary. He at first respected this about her leadership but had slowly come to resent how little attention she paid to his side of the organization. HR was the last thing on her mind, and she constantly reminded James that he was solely accountable for the talent side. He felt like he was to be seen but not heard most days at Driftwell.

Unlike Anna, James had undergraduate and master's degrees in industrial and organizational psychology. He was beginning to question some of the more recent leadership decisions made by both Anna and Graham. If he were honest, he didn't disagree with the anonymous post, but he dared not voice it out loud.

As James exited Anna's office, she turned to Graham, shut her laptop, and leaned in. "Okay, you have my attention. What is this acquisition you want to make?"

Anna knew something had to change. Their core customer base was shrinking. AI was looming in the background, and no one had a good idea what the technology would do to the business. She just knew they had to get ahead of it. Or at least, that's what she heard loud and clear coming out of the last board meeting.

"I was with our investor community a few weeks back. They made it resoundingly clear that we need to move from simply being a biotech company to being an AI-enabled biotech company. Companies that are crossing this AI valuation bridge are seeing a 2×–3× on their valuations."

"But Graham, we can't just flip a switch and become an AI company overnight. Aren't we talking years of investment and R&D? And where do you think that funding is going to come from?" Anna's lack of sleep was coming through in her tone.

"There is a new AI startup led by an up-and-coming founder named Priya. She just made the cover of *Fast Company* last month. She's developed a new large language model specifically for the biotech industry. It's going to help us not only move faster but also tell the AI story to our investor community. Her startup could be key for us crossing that AI valuation bridge."

Anna reopened her laptop and went to the *Fast Company* site. She saw Priya, who looked like a recent college graduate, sparkling with a smile on the magazine cover. *Ugh, these kids have no clue what it actually takes to build a business*, Anna thought. *Must be nice*.

She looked into the distance, contemplating this acquisition and picturing adding Priya to her coveted leadership team. "Do we have the cash flow for this? Do you think it's a good deal?"

"Listen, Anna. This is never going to be cheaper. We need to get this while it's still in development. They need the cash to keep building, and we need the AI story to keep growing. It's really a win-win." Anna nervously clicked her pen a few times as she considered this.

She let out a long sigh. "Alright, make it happen. Make sure to let James know as he will have to manage the merging of the cultures. And I want a meeting with Priya ASAP. I need to make sure she and I can work together."

Graham leaped up from his chair, excited that this was a much easier discussion than he had prepped for. "On it."

Anna returned to the anonymous post on Reddit. Why was this getting under her skin? It wasn't the first time someone accused her of greed. But something about the poem—its discrete mocking—felt different. It was like hearing a truth she'd worked years to silence.

James got word of the AI startup acquisition through the grapevine. He pinged Anna to confirm whether the rumors were true. A few hours later, she sent back a thumbs-up emoji.

Always the last to know, James thought.

He initiated a background check on Priya and was surprised to see what came back. Apparently, she'd left her PhD early and was on bad terms with a top professor at Stanford. Her references were lukewarm, and some even cautioned on her leadership approach. The most concerning was a comment from her former co-founder: *She may present as laid back on the surface, but she's vicious behind closed doors.*

James raised these concerns with Anna in the break room when no one else was around. She'd become increasingly difficult to pin down. Surprising James, she brushed the concerns off quickly.

"James, I've met her and she is exactly what this company needs right now. I am sure her former co-founder is just bitter and jealous since they left before the big acquisition."

James bit his lip, wanting to press the issue. But Anna had already turned around and was heading back to her office, seemingly unfazed by the red flags.

From the hallway, he heard her shout back in his direction, "And don't give up on that Reddit poet James. We need accountability for those actions." Her voice trailed as she turned the corner.

Commentary: But Leaders Do Care

I am convinced that most leaders care deeply about people. They are human, after all, meaning they too are biologically wired to connect, to empathize, to belong. Business, at its best, can be a remarkable force for good: it gives people purpose and fair pay, meets customer needs, and leaves communities stronger than it found them.

But somewhere along the way, something startling happened. Over the past fifty years, corporate lifespans have shrunk, creating instability for the people and places that depend on them. EY research shows that a company's lifespan on the S&P500 was 67 years in the 1940s; today, that number is down to 15 years.[7] To make matters worse, toxic leadership behaviors have fueled a post-pandemic mental-health crisis. An unrelenting obsession with automation and the valuations that come with it has begun to replace livelihoods with algorithms.

Somewhere along the way, we lost the plot of what business is all about. Like all things that matter deeply, losing our way is complex—full of human emotion, ambition, and contradiction. And as the old saying goes, the road to hell is paved with good intentions.

The modern work life, whom many describe as a hellscape, wasn't meant to be this way. When Milton Friedman wrote in his 1970 *New York Times Magazine* essay that "there is one and only one social responsibility of business—to use its resources and engage in activities designed to increase its profits,"[8] he stripped business of moral obligation. He declared the enterprise amoral. *I doubt he imagined the unbridled pursuit of profit that would follow or the human cost it would leave behind.*

That single idea—that a business could be amoral—gave generations of leaders permission to separate personal conscience from corporate decision-making. The end (profit) justified any means. And the means, over time, came at the expense of humanity.

Before we grab our pitchforks and blame Friedman for everything, it's worth noting that the shareholder landscape he described looked very different from what it does today. In 1971, roughly 60% of listed stock was owned by individuals. Today, according to *Forbes*, the wealthiest 10% of Americans own 93% of the stock market's value.[9] In practice, that ownership rarely shows up as a person. It shows up as institutional funds, index benchmarks, and quarterly performance targets. Take a typical index fund: it may hold shares in thousands of companies, governed by rules and algorithms rather than human judgment. The "shareholder" has become a faceless institution, a fund, a mathematical entity.

Then, in the 1970s, came another idea that cemented the problem into the very architecture of business education. Economists Michael Jensen and William Meckling took Friedman's premise and codified it into orthodoxy. They called it *agency theory*, and it became the cornerstone of every MBA curriculum that followed.[10] You may remember it being mentioned in Anna and Graham's lecture.

The theory was deceptively simple. They agreed with Milton that a company exists to maximize shareholder value. But since people can't always be trusted to do that, they must be watched, measured, and incentivized. The assumption was that employees, left to their own devices, wouldn't work hard or make the right choices unless financially motivated or closely controlled.

So, companies built systems, including incentives, scorecards, and surveillance tools, to make sure employees acted in shareholders' interests, even if that meant trusting them less. As agency theory took hold, another shift occurred. In the 1970s, CEO pay was mostly salary and bonus. Equity was minimal. But if leaders were to act like shareholders, the logic went, their pay should mirror shareholder returns. The results were staggering. From 1978 to today, CEO compensation has risen over 1,000%, while typical worker pay has grown around 24%.[11]

Hot Take: It Is the Responsibility of Leaders to Care for Their People

I remember my time at one of the world's largest consulting firms, leading research on human capital. I wrote a piece urging executives to consider the impact of declining employee engagement as they pursued aggressive cost-cutting. A respected colleague left a single comment in the review: "*I don't agree with this argument. Business leaders have responsibility only to profits, not the wellbeing of people.*"

That sentence has haunted me ever since. And to be clear, the person who wrote this was absolutely lovely to work with. This wasn't your typical consulting partner. They were soft-spoken and kind, and super ambitious; a lot like Anna in her early years. But this person reflected a mindset produced by decades of one-dimensional business education—an MBA stripped of moral imagination. Why worry about people if profits rise? Employees are listed as costs, not assets, on the balance sheet. They should be grateful, we're told, just to have a job.

That piece I wrote sparked an internal debate that reached the C-suite at the company I was with. We found ourselves asking: *Is "do no harm" really enough for businesses? Does business have a deeper duty to the people behind the profits?*

Here's the uncomfortable truth we came to in the room that day: even when we say we're doing no harm in business, we often are. We pollute the environment. We lay off workers. We label human consequences as "externalities." And then we do what business does best. We quantify it, assign it a dollar value, and move on.

But this, my friends, is losing the plot. Business was never meant to be morally neutral. It was meant to build, to serve, to create value that lifts everyone it touches. Yes, shareholders matter, but so do workers, customers, suppliers, and the communities that make business possible.

Profit is not the enemy. Amnesia is.

> **It's time we remember why we built businesses in the first place, not merely to extract value, but to create it. To measure success not just by what we earn, but by what we contribute and create.**

The Research: What Is the Purpose of Business?

In management scholarship, there's a question that has echoed through classrooms and boardrooms for more than a century—a kind of academic analogy posed to those who study the role of enterprise in society:

"Justice is to law, as medicine is to health, as business is to ______?"[12]

It's deceptively simple, but profound in its implications. If law's purpose is to pursue justice, and medicine's purpose is to restore health, then what, exactly, is the purpose of business?

This riddle appears in management literature throughout the twentieth century, as scholars debated what a firm is ultimately for. As I describe in *How Behavioral Economics Influences Management*,[13] the question became a philosophical counterweight to the rise of shareholder primacy. Economists such as Adolf Berle argued in 1931 that corporations exist to serve shareholders, while Merrick Dodd countered that they also bear obligations to employees, customers, and the wider community.

Later thinkers would expand this debate, suggesting that the true purpose of business is not profit itself but the creation of prosperity and flourishing, an outcome in which people, organizations, and societies thrive together. As the text notes, this analogy forces us to confront the deeper moral dimension of commerce: just as justice gives meaning to law and health gives direction to medicine, business, too, must orient toward something beyond its mechanics of exchange.

The most enduring answer to that riddle? Business is to **prosperity**.

Profit may fuel the system, but it was never meant to be the purpose. The purpose is to make life better. It's to build, to serve, to leave things improved because business exists at all. The real question is how we broaden our understanding of business, so it captures prosperity, not just profit.

The scholars who first posed this riddle offered four ways to rethink business in pursuit of shared prosperity and to counter the drift we see today.

The Moral Architecture of Modern Capitalism

1. **Reframed the purpose of business.** It is *not to maximize shareholder value, but to optimize collective value*, which includes all the good created for employees, customers, communities, and society, minus the harm caused. Profit is one expression of value, but not the only one. True success lies in maximizing the net positive impact of business activity across everyone it touches.
2. **Expanded accountability.** Business, they wrote, is responsible to all who are affected by its actions across time and space. Looking through the lens of past, present, and future widens accountability beyond shareholders to workers, suppliers, customers, communities, and even generations not yet born. Decisions ripple outward, shaping lives and ecosystems long after quarterly reports are forgotten.

3. **Drew a moral boundary around control.** Business must never violate human dignity. Every participant, whether a factory worker, software engineer, or contract cleaner, deserves respect as an end in themselves, not merely a means to efficiency. Governance, incentives, and culture must protect that basic dignity.
4. **Redefined success.** Financial performance matters, but it isn't the whole story. The test of a thriving business is how much it contributes to human flourishing while safeguarding dignity along the way. Profit, innovation, and community renewal are all paths to success, but each must serve this larger purpose.

Together, these four ideas form a moral architecture sturdy enough to hold the weight of modern capitalism. They challenge the narrow shareholder doctrine that dominated the past half-century and replace it with a more human standard. If law is for justice and medicine is for health, then business, at its best, is for the creation of collective value, the art of turning ambition into shared prosperity without sacrificing the people who make it possible.

The problem, of course, is that collective value is difficult to measure. Shareholder returns can be tracked by the minute; prosperity can't be charted on a Bloomberg screen. And what we don't measure, we stop managing.

Measuring What Matters One of the oldest truths in management is also the most overlooked: what we measure, we focus on. For decades, business measurement has revolved around a narrow axis of shareholder returns. The balance sheet became our moral compass because it was an easy way to measure success. Earnings per share became the language of value. And, over time, the metrics we used began to shape the behaviors we rewarded. When profit is the only measure that counts, everything else—people, purpose, community—eventually becomes invisible. But what we fail to measure, we fail to manage.

At the beginning of this act I shared about the consulting company and the exercise that ensued about whether a company is okay with simply "do not harm." I was at Accenture at the time, and the leaders believed deeply that businesses could do better than simply "do not harm." So, when Accenture launched its 360° Value framework in 2021, it wasn't just a branding exercise. It was a recognition that, if business is to remain legitimate in the twenty-first century, it must find new ways to define success. Their approach measures six dimensions of value—financial, client, talent, inclusion and diversity, sustainability, and what they call "custom value" tailored to each stakeholder group.[14]

The name itself—*360° Value*—captures something profound: that business operates in a full circle of stakeholders, not a straight line from investor to return. It took years to create and numerous PhD data scientists to ensure it was ready to go head-to-head with the longstanding profit metrics.

In the traditional model, financial outcomes sat at the top, and everything else was subordinate. But in this expanded model, profit becomes one dimension among many, not the sole purpose of enterprise. It's a recognition that businesses are living systems, interconnected, adaptive, and dependent on trust, people, and the planet that sustains them.

This shift matters deeply because measurement drives attention, and attention drives culture. When leaders start quantifying inclusion, sustainability, and employee well-being with the same rigor as revenue growth, priorities begin to realign. New conversations emerge in boardrooms. Incentives begin to shift. Suddenly, the invisible becomes visible.

Accenture's framework doesn't reject profit; it reframes it. It argues that long-term prosperity depends on balancing multiple forms of value—not just financial gain, but also human, social, and environmental health. Profits can only be sustained when individuals and communities prosper.

And that's the lesson for every organization wrestling with its purpose. If we truly believe business exists to create collective value, then we must learn to measure collective value, to give form to what we claim to care about. Because history has taught us that the moment we start measuring what matters, businesses begin to change.

Reflective Exercise: When Purpose Goes Missing

According to Gallup research, 41% of American workers cannot clearly articulate their organization's purpose.[15] Nearly half of the workforce has no idea what makes their company distinct—or why it exists beyond turning a profit.

And let's be honest: the blunt reality of "*maximizing shareholder wealth*" isn't exactly the kind of purpose that gets people out of bed on a Monday morning.

I remember attending a team meeting early in my career led by someone I deeply admired—a senior leader who had earned his PhD in Business from Harvard. I thought, *How incredible it must be to have been trained at one of the best business schools in the world.* I showed up that day eager to absorb whatever wisdom he might share, hoping that just being in the same room might spark some of his brilliance to rub off on me.

He began the meeting by expressing concern about the team's health. The quality of our work, he said, had started to slip, and he suspected that the long hours—the sixty-plus-hour weeks that had become routine in consulting—were taking a toll. He paused, giving us a moment of hope that maybe, just maybe, he was about to say something human.

Then he concluded with words that sucked the air out of the room:

> *"Don't forget," he said, "the only reason you are here is to make the partners of this firm rich. You won't get wealthy working here, so don't kill yourself trying. You'll make a good, honest living, but never forget the purpose of this company—to maximize profits for the partners. Your focus is to do good enough work to keep this job."*

Silence followed. A few people laughed nervously, thinking it was a joke. But it wasn't. His statement was completely sincere and, in his mind, entirely logical.

I sat there stunned. This was a person trained at one of the most prestigious institutions in the world, yet even he could not imagine a vision of business larger than enriching those at the top. It struck me that this wasn't just an individual belief. It was a worldview; one deeply embedded in our systems of education and leadership.

At that moment, I realized how easy it is for a business to lose its soul when purpose is reduced to profit. When leaders can't articulate why their organization exists beyond making money, people eventually stop bringing their full selves to work. They comply, but they don't commit. They perform, but they don't believe.

Take a few moments to reflect, either personally or with your team:

1. Can you clearly state the purpose of your organization in one sentence—without mentioning profit or shareholder return?
2. What would you tell a new employee on their first day about *why* your company exists?
3. If your organization disappeared tomorrow, what would the world lose?

Write down your answers. Notice whether they come easily or require effort. The gap between what you *say* and what you *measure* often reveals where purpose has gone missing.

When people no longer know *why* they work, even the best strategy won't save a company. Purpose isn't a slogan; it's the oxygen your workers need to perform at their best. Without it, every business eventually suffocates under the sole pursuit of profits.

Scene 3: Startup Mode

Flashback

Anna had taken the helm of Driftwell during the heat of the pandemic. Demand for biotech had exploded as government money flooded the sector, chasing anything that promised to blunt the effects of COVID-19. It was a strange, heady time—equal parts anxiety and euphoria—as scientists, executives, and investors united around a single goal: saving the world and making history.

But with the gold rush came competition. Barriers to entry fell. In a single year, more than 115 biotech companies went public. Growth looked limitless, until it didn't.

Anna knew the surge was temporary, but she'd earned the CEO job by promising the board an *aggressive five-year growth plan*. And that plan would require a partner she could trust.

The moment the offer came through, she called Graham, her closest ally from graduate school. He had done exactly what he'd set out to do—he was next in line for CFO at a major tech company. If she wanted him, she'd have to make an offer he couldn't refuse.

She took a deep breath and dialed.

"Graham, it's Anna."

"Anna? Oh my God—you got the job, didn't you?" His excitement made her smile.

"You beat me to it. How did you know?"

"I knew the minute we met in that economics class you'd end up running something big. Congratulations. It must feel incredible."

"It does," she said softly. Then, more firmly: "And I want you with me. Come to Driftwell. Be my CFO."

There was silence on the other end. Graham leaned back in his chair, calculating. He was about eighteen months away from the CFO role at his current firm. Three years from full vesting. Anna's offer could hit his financial target two years faster and added the bonus of doing something meaningful.

"Graham, are you still there?"

He chuckled. "For once, I'm actually speechless." He could hear Anna clicking her pen. It was a nervous tic she'd had since business school.

"Let's do lunch next week," he said. "I want to see the books."

"Deal. But I'm picking the place this time. No more pizza joints."

"Hey, I'm just thinking like an owner," he teased. "Keeping expenses down."

Graham laughed, though part of him wondered when they'd both become so obsessed with numbers.

The following week, they met over lunch. Anna came armed with a printed deck—a sharp, color-coded five-year growth plan. She slid it across the table like a poker hand she was sure would win.

Graham skimmed it, his brow tightening.

"What?" Anna asked. "Why that face?"

"Anna, the plan's ambitious, but you've got a cost problem. You've given out so much equity it's depressing the stock. I don't want to be the guy who comes in and starts clawing that back."

Anna didn't flinch. "Then we make the tough calls. People understand. The pandemic reminded everyone what matters, right? Family, health. . . not stock options." Graham studied her. He didn't remember her being this detached from reality. At his current company, employees had become *more* entitled to perks, not less. But she seemed to genuinely believe it, and in the end, he took the job.

■ ■ ■

August 15, 2024

Powerful Duo Acquires Rising Founder's AI Startup

It was exactly the *Fortune* cover Anna had pictured back in graduate school. She just hadn't imagined sharing it with Graham. Still, without him, the acquisition would never have happened.

When Anna met Priya for the first time, she was a little awe-struck. Priya was, in many ways, everything Anna wasn't. She moved through conversations with an easy, laid-back confidence, yet her work carried an intensity that was unmatched. She told story after story of all-nighters and pushing her team to make the impossible possible.

Graham noticed the shift almost immediately. Anna began using startup language and adopting a founder mentality, slipping borrowed phrases into conversations that felt like they came from Priya's world. It didn't sound entirely natural coming from her, but she was smiling for the first time in a long while, and he didn't want to dim that light.

Still, the dynamics had shifted. Priya's presence energized Anna, but it stirred something else in Graham—an awareness that the stakes of his decisions were even higher now.

He had been one of the most bullish voices championing the acquisition when the macro environment was still roaring. In a market that rewarded speed and bold bets on AI, their move had felt obvious. Anna had trusted his conviction, and he'd carried that trust with pride.

But as conditions tightened and capital grew more cautious, he felt a nagging fear he didn't want to name: they might have overpaid. And Driftwell was beginning to feel the strain.

The numbers told the truth. Priya's AI acquisition was burning through cash, and Driftwell was running out of runway. He knew he had to bring it to Anna, not to deflate her excitement, but because she deserved honesty.

"Expenses have to come down," he told her flatly. "The clearest place to start is equity. We've been too generous, and investors are raising questions. We talked about this when I first saw the books."

Anna looked at him, really looked, and he felt the familiar steadiness in her gaze. "Graham, are you sure there isn't another option? I don't love walking back a decision I made less than a year ago."

She wasn't challenging him. She was checking the ground beneath them, making sure he had scanned every angle, every implication. This was how she led: direct, principled, careful.

"I've run every scenario," he said. "This is the least painful path."

Anna nodded slowly. Not because it was the answer she wanted, but because she trusted him. She always had. Even now, in a market that rewarded second-guessing and fear, that trust felt like the thread holding everything together.

"Okay," she said finally. "Then we'll do it. I'll get James to schedule an all-employee town hall next week where we will make the announcement." She sounded somewhat defeated but quickly moved on to the pile of printouts on her desk.

And in that moment, despite the downturn and the growing weight of the acquisition, something between them settled. They were still on the same side.

■ ■ ■

When Anna suggested an all-employee town hall, Graham assumed she would prepare the workforce for austerity. He spent the night before writing her talking points. No doubt, the next year or two were going to be bumpy, and Graham was hopeful that Anna would set the stage for tough decisions ahead. Instead, she delivered more of a rally cry.

"Starting today," she said brightly, "we're moving into *startup mode*. Priya's team has shown us what's possible when people act like founders—long hours, full commitment, all in. That's the culture we're building here. We will change the world together, but only if you think like an owner of this company."

Graham's stomach dropped. He knew a company-wide equity freeze would take place by the end of the week. Why would she tell people to "think like owners" when their ownership was about to vanish?

Anna left the stage energized, convinced the room was with her. She saw inspiration where Graham saw panic. "They're hungry again," she told him later. "Who doesn't want to work at a startup? That's where the magic happens."

Moments later, Graham was storming down the hallway after her. He caught her just before she reached her office.

"Anna, we need to talk." He shut the door behind him, hard enough to make her jump.

"What the hell was that?" he demanded. "Why would you say that right before we freeze equity?"

Anna blinked, caught off guard by the anger in his voice. "Graham, people need motivation. We're reigniting our purpose."

"Motivation?" He ran a hand through his hair. "You just told four thousand employees to act like owners, right before we take away their ownership." His tone shifted from anger to exasperation.

Anna stared at him, unshaken. "You're overreacting. That is for James in HR to take care of, not you."

He exhaled, defeated. "You've lost touch, Anna. They're not founders. They're people barely getting by these days."

She looked back at him, a flicker of pity crossing her face. *He's softer than I remember*, she thought.

At that moment, Graham had a decision to make. If he were to remain CFO, he'd have to let go of the people's side of the business. Anna was right, his job was to make the numbers work, and he was damn good at that.

Outside, the buzz of office life carried on, but the inherent spark was fading quickly.

By the afternoon, the anonymous Reddit thread had already begun anew.

"Anyone else think that town hall was completely out to lunch?"

The comments lit up fast with sarcasm, frustration, and disbelief. Graham read enough to know where it was heading. Driftwell's own internal watercooler Slack channel began to mirror a similar sentiment. He sent a quick note to Comms: "*Let's temporarily pause executive access to the water cooler Slack thread until the temperature cools.*"

There was no need for Anna to see the harsh truth. The delta of her perception and the workers' day-to-day reality was too far. Driftwell had already departed from the story she was still telling.

He closed his laptop and stared out the window, the city lights flickering as the sun began to set. The office noise had faded to a dull whirr, but the unease lingered.

Driftwell would show growth again on paper after the equity cuts, but Graham could feel the foundation shifting beneath them. He felt a widening gap between the story they told investors and the one their people were living on the inside. That gap, he knew, would eventually rear its ugly head.

By the time the first headlines would appear a year later—***"Private Equity Firm Calls for CEO's Removal"***—it wouldn't come as a shock to him. The cracks had been there all along. He had just stopped pointing them out.

Commentary: The Refounding Illusion

What's happening within Driftwell isn't an outlier; it's a blueprint. In the months that followed the public debut of generative AI, I watched versions of this same story unfold across industries. Boards demanded AI roadmaps. CEOs announced "second foundings." Executives rebranded mature companies as startups overnight. Each believed they were reigniting their purpose, but what they were really doing was rehearsing Driftwell's script: mistaking pressure for passion and performance optics for truth.

Belief can be intoxicating, especially when you sit close enough to the power source to feel its heat. Every leader wants to believe their passion is contagious. That conviction will cascade down the hierarchy like sunlight through glass. But sunlight bends. By the time it reaches the lower floors, it's often filtered, distorted, or completely lost.

The Korn Ferry *Motivation Meter* makes that distortion visible.[16] Eighty-one percent of CEOs say they're willing to go "above and beyond" at work. Among employees without management responsibilities, only 57% feel the same way—the lowest level recorded since 2019. Even middle managers, once the emotional bridge between vision and execution, have seen motivation slip from 76% to 73% in the past year. This may not sound like a lot on the surface, but it is.

The gap isn't just statistical, it's also psychological. Senior leaders operate with autonomy, access, and a sense of ownership that naturally fuels drive. They see the horizon. They have levers to pull. For many employees, those levers don't exist. They only experience metrics, mandates, and meetings that feel increasingly disconnected from meaning.

This is where the "refounding" illusion takes hold. From the C-suite, rebranding as a *startup* feels bold, visionary, heroic. From the workforce, it often feels tone-deaf to another demand for energy without equity. Leaders call it a reset; employees call it déjà vu.

Motivation isn't a universal constant; it's context-dependent. What sparks purpose for one group can spark resentment for another. When leaders talk about *acting like founders*, they're drawing on experiences of agency, risk-taking, and ownership. Which, let's be clear, are privileges not equally distributed across an organization.

It's easy for leaders to confuse their *view* of reality with reality itself. It's the empathy blind spot of modern business: assuming that belief at the top equals belief everywhere. But when the story you're telling doesn't match the story people are living, belief becomes performance, and performance eventually becomes delusion.

The result? Organizations that look energized from above but are silently eroding below. Charts rise, engagement falls. The narrative sounds triumphant; the hallway chatter tells another truth.

At Driftwell, Anna wasn't wrong to seek belief; every leader needs a story to rally around. But she mistook her own performance narrative and energy for moral clarity. She thought motivation could be declared into existence without doing the harder work of changing the system itself.

It can't. Motivation isn't built in the boardroom; it's built in the spaces between people. It exists in trust, in fairness, in the daily proof that someone's work still matters. When that proof disappears, the story collapses. And by the time leaders realize they've lost the plot, it's too late because no one's listening to it anymore.

Hot Take: A Startup Mindset Is an Excuse for Chaos

In the wake of the AI gold rush, nearly every company I knew went into what they called "startup mode," even though most were well-established, publicly traded firms. Suddenly, seasoned executives began talking like founders. They adopted the vocabulary of hustle: speed, grit, disruption. Office lobbies displayed banners reading "Startup Mode," and all-hands emails declared this "the company's rebirth."

I witnessed one of these movements firsthand. I was invited into a company to provide research advisory services and was deeply embedded in their culture. I'll never forget the moment the CEO stood before employees and announced, "From this day forward, we act like founders and owners." The promise was intoxicating: rebuild the company from the ground up, become an "AI-first organization," and share in the wealth when the refounding succeeded.

At first, energy spiked. Long nights were celebrated, weekends blurred, and urgency became a virtue. But the enthusiasm wasn't evenly distributed. Most employees held little or no equity, so "ownership" was purely symbolic. Within months, the glow faded. Projects stalled, talent left, and frustration crept into every town hall. Yet, instead of examining the system, leadership blamed the people. Behind closed doors, they began saying the quiet part out loud: "*Some just don't care enough.*"

Turnover climbed to record highs. Entire departments were restructured and then restructured again as the CEO cycled through direct reports searching for believers. They were looking for those "wired" for the new AI era. The irony was almost painful. The company's real problem wasn't a lack of motivation. It was the culture itself. Over the course of six months, most had lost trust, clarity had eroded, and there was an absence of a shared purpose beyond chasing the next valuation narrative.

No one at the top paused to ask the deeper questions. Maybe it wasn't the people who'd lost their edge. Maybe it was the *system* that had lost its soul. Perhaps it wasn't apathy at all, but exhaustion from a leadership story that had lost its plot.

It was, in every way, a living example of the self-serving bias. Leaders interpret their own urgency as vision, and their employees' fatigue as a sign of failure. To be clear, a self-serving bias is not intentional deceit; it's how the mind works without self-awareness and guardrails. Our brains instinctively protect the self, crafting stories that keep us in the right.

The Research: What Causes the Drift from a Shared Reality?

The Mirror Problem I've spent years sitting in rooms with executives who are convinced their people just don't care as much as they do. Behind closed doors with me, leaders lament the lack of work ethic and drive in their workforce. The conversation usually starts the same way: "*We've got a motivation problem.*" The tone carries both frustration and disbelief, as if, somewhere along the chain of command, the organization's pulse simply stopped. We rarely start with a self-reflection on leadership, culture, or even organizational design.

When I ask these same leaders what keeps them motivated, the answers are almost poetic. "*I believe in our mission.*" "*I love building things that matter.*" "*I'm driven by purpose.*" "*I am a natural builder and leader.*" Then I ask what they think motivates their teams. Without hesitation, the responses are always extrinsic: "*Bonuses.*" "*Titles.*" "*Recognition.*"

That's the mirror problem. Leaders see themselves through a wide-angle lens, describing their own motivations as complex, purposeful, and deeply human. But they see others through a narrow frame of transactional incentives. They see anyone other than a leader being motivated to work for that paycheck, for the time off, or the need for benefits.

That's when I started noticing something deeper than an organizational behavior problem. It wasn't just systems that were outdated (it certainly doesn't help), but I discovered it was the mental models leaders were using to understand their teams.

I play a clip of the movie *Office Space* in one of my keynote presentations, because one line captures the modern workplace better than most research papers. The main character, Peter, sums up his disengagement by saying, "It's not that I'm lazy. It's just that I don't care." It's both funny and tragic. Most employees aren't apathetic by nature. They've just stopped believing their effort changes anything. The underlying inequity between those who lead and those who don't seems too great to close. And without that equity compensation to financially align with going all out for shareholders, many employees choose to do what's needed to get by. It's ironically the most rational response.

It's what researchers call the *motivation perception gap*—the space between what leaders *think* drives people and what actually does. A large MIT Sloan study found that executives ranked compensation and performance incentives as the top motivators for their workforce, while employees placed purpose, flexibility, and recognition at the top of their lists. In other words, each group assumed the other valued what they themselves valued least. The result is a silent misunderstanding that slowly erodes trust.

This gap doesn't just distort how leaders design incentives; it reshapes how they interpret behavior. When an employee hesitates to volunteer for a new project, a leader may assume disengagement, when in truth the employee is overwhelmed or doesn't find the project meaningful. When leaders celebrate profit milestones, employees may feel invisible if their personal contributions aren't acknowledged. Over time, this misalignment compounds as leaders double down on metrics, while teams privately withdraw.

What's most striking is that this perception gap is not born of apathy, but of assumption. Leaders genuinely believe they're motivating their teams, just as employees genuinely believe their leaders are out of touch. It's a mirror of our own cognitive bias, which sees the world not as it is, but as we are.

A Self-Serving Power Paradox Psychology gives us language for what's happening beneath the surface of leadership, beyond just a perception gap. One of the clearest explanations is the *self-serving bias*, which is our brain's instinct to take credit for success, but shift blame for failure. When things go well, we attribute it to our intelligence, discipline, or strategic genius. When things go poorly, we blame the market, the team, or the timing. It's a subtle act of self-preservation, the ego's way of staying intact.

In leadership, this bias doesn't fade; it multiplies. As people rise, their decisions gain greater visibility, and their confidence deepens. Feedback grows more filtered, and power begins to dull self-awareness. Studies in organizational psychology show that status and authority amplify self-serving attributions, widening the gap between how leaders see themselves and how others experience their leadership.

Social psychologist Adam Galinsky and his colleagues once ran a deceptively simple experiment that revealed just how profoundly power reshapes perception.[17] He and his team asked participants to imagine themselves in positions of authority and then perform a basic task: draw the letter E with their finger on their forehead so that another person could read it. Those primed with power overwhelmingly used their finger to draw the E in a way that made sense to *themselves*—not to the observer.

It was a small gesture, but it captured something massive about leadership: the more power we hold, the harder it becomes to see the world through someone else's eyes. Galinsky called this the "power and perspective gap." The people at the top aren't necessarily uncaring; they're just less likely to realize that their view isn't universal.

Building on that insight, researcher Nathanael Fast and his colleagues explored how power also changes how we interpret feedback.[18] In one study, managers were asked to evaluate their employees' willingness to speak up. The more powerful the manager felt, the less likely they were to view employee feedback as valuable, and the more likely they were to see silence as alignment. Fast's follow-up studies found that power inflates self-confidence, dulls curiosity, and makes leaders less likely to seek input. Ironically, those who need feedback the most are the ones who stop asking for it.

Put together, these studies illustrate how leadership drift happens not in moments of failure, but in moments of certainty. The more confident we become in our own perspective, the less we notice when others stop sharing theirs. Very few leadership teams at the top receive and listen to feedback from those below them.

At Driftwell, this science came to life in real time. The leadership team wasn't made up of scoundrels; they were simply powerful people who had stopped realizing how their perspective had narrowed. Surrounded by affirmation, they mistook agreement for alignment. Feedback loops closed, empathy thinned, and overconfidence took root. The more convinced they became that they were leading with vision, the less they noticed the growing silence around them. You saw this when Graham determined the best path forward was not to give voice to areas outside his lane.

One of the most fascinating insights into this dynamic comes from social psychologist Dacher Keltner, who coined what he calls *the power paradox*.[19] His decades of research show that people often *earn* power through qualities like empathy, collaboration, and fairness—yet once they have it, those same qualities begin to erode. In other words, the very traits that helped someone rise become harder to access once they're at the top. Power literally changes how people think and behave, rewiring the brain to prioritize one's own perspective over others.

Keltner's team demonstrated this phenomenon through what became known as the "Cookie Monster Experiment."[20] In the study, three people were placed in a room and asked to complete a task together. Midway through, a plate of four cookies was brought in—one more than each person could take evenly. Time and again, the person randomly assigned as the "leader" of the group took the extra cookie. They not only claimed the additional reward but also often ate it more loudly and messily than the others. The finding was both comical and unsettling: even arbitrary power triggers a sense of entitlement and a loss of self-regulation.

This is the subtle drift of leadership. The same person who once stayed late to help a teammate now assumes others should sacrifice for the cause. The CEO who says, "*I'm working late because I care*" later concludes, "*They burned out because they couldn't keep up.*" Both statements feel true from the inside, and that's the danger. Bias doesn't feel like ego; it feels like clarity.

Over time, these small distortions add up. Leaders stop noticing when the story they tell themselves about their company no longer aligns with the one their people are living. The distance grows slowly, almost imperceptibly, until one day they look up and realize they've been leading from a completely different reality.

The distance caused by power widens the gap between perception and reality, between intention and impact. At Driftwell, as in many real organizations, the leadership team didn't wake up one day deciding to lose its way; they simply stopped seeing clearly.

None of us is immune. The human brain is wired for self-preservation. It filters information in ways that protect the ego, not the system. That's why even well-intentioned leaders can drift away from reality and why the first act of regaining the plot isn't a strategy, but a mindset shift.

Reflective Exercise: Returning to Curiosity

Start with this perspective: *Assume the story you're telling yourself might be incomplete*. It sounds simple, but it's the one habit that separates leaders who evolve from those who remain stuck.

The next time something goes wrong—attrition spikes, a project misses its mark, engagement scores dip—pause before you explain why. Write down your first instinctive explanation. Then ask: What if my view isn't the full story? What forces outside my control shaped this outcome? What part did the system play that I may be overlooking?

And if you have a trusted advisor, share your reflection with them. This is why coaching becomes essential the higher you go. Most leaders don't lack skill or competence. What they lack is self-awareness, the ability to see how their behavior ripples through the system and shapes the very outcomes they're trying to change.

If drift begins when leaders stop seeing clearly, then rediscovery begins when they start asking better questions. Curiosity is the simplest, most powerful way to reconnect with reality, and yet it's often the first thing to disappear as leaders rise. As I often tell leaders, curiosity is both the compass and the mirror of leadership. It points us toward what we don't yet know and reflects what we may have forgotten about ourselves.

So, before rushing into the next meeting or decision, pause and reflect on the following:

1. **What am I no longer curious about?**

   Think about the areas of your business or team that you no longer question. What processes, assumptions, or relationships have become too familiar to notice? Curiosity fades where certainty grows too comfortable.

2. **When was the last time I changed my mind?**

   Leaders who can't recall the last time they changed a perspective may be mistaking confidence for clarity. True curiosity invites the possibility of being wrong not as failure, but as a sign of growth.

3. **What questions am I afraid to ask?**

   The best leaders know that curiosity often feels risky. What question, if asked honestly, might challenge your narrative, your metrics, or your comfort? Write it down. Then ask it.

4. **Who tells me the truth, even when it's uncomfortable?**

   Every leader needs someone who's willing to say, "You're missing something." If you can't name that person, you may already be drifting.

5. **What am I seeing only from my own vantage point?**

   Take Galinsky's experiment to heart—imagine how your decisions look from the floor, not the boardroom. Curiosity means putting the E on your forehead the right way for others to read.

Leadership isn't about having all the answers. It's about staying awake to the questions that matter most. Curiosity keeps us tethered to our shared humanity. The part of us that still listens, still learns, still wonders. Before you can lead others well, you have to lead yourself back to wonder.

Curiosity is contagious. Leaders who cultivate curiosity and practice self-reflection begin to build cultures that do the same. Teams start speaking up earlier. Patterns surface faster. The work becomes less about defending positions and more about discovering reality. Over time, that's how organizations regain the plot with one honest reflection at a time.

So, ask yourself: *When was the last time I was truly curious about the people I lead?*

Scene 4: The Strategic Reset

One week after the board meeting opening scene, August 11, 2025

The office was somber. Not just because it was 5 a.m., but because of *why* everyone was there.

Fifteen HR business partners and their legal counterparts sat around the long conference table, stuffing thick manila folders. Inside: outplacement service brochures, COBRA forms, and a stack of legal documents to sign away the noise. The folders landed in piles with soft, terminal thuds.

James stood by the window watching the city's skyline awaken. He had fought hard to advocate for a complete six-month severance package for those impacted, something decent that he could justify. But Graham's numbers had won. Only eight weeks. The spreadsheet had prevailed over clemency.

His thoughts drifted to Priya and her team. The acquisition promised to transform Driftwell into an AI-first company, where the sky was the limit. Instead, it had drained their cash, their credibility, and his patience. Her "Silicon Valley Visionary" energy clashed with the company's biotech roots, and her obsession with machine learning had alienated both investors and staff. *"AI is the future,"* she said. *"People are just slow to see it."*

Anna's voice replaying in his mind from last night's call, calm, almost maternal.

"James, people get laid off all the time. They'll land on their feet. Some even end up better off."

She meant to sound reassuring. It landed as callous.

He rubbed his eyes. The coffee had gone cold an hour ago.

"How many more folders?" he asked, voice low.

"Another hundred," someone replied. "We'll be done in thirty minutes."

He nodded, though he wasn't really listening. The clock ticked toward six. In less than an hour, an all-company email would hit inboxes announcing the "organizational reset." By seven, IT would send individualized emails to unaware employees. Some safe, some not. There would be no conversation or 1:1 to notify in person. Just an email with a subject line that changed lives.

James had written that first draft himself. He stared at the email on his screen. It looked sterile, corporate. It had to be. Half the workforce was remote, so they'd done what leaders do when humanity doesn't scale: they automated it.

He'd set up war rooms across the building for his HR function to work from. Small teams huddled in conference rooms, ready to take calls, answer questions, and absorb the grief from the unfortunate souls impacted.

Every system was in place.

Every word had been reviewed by legal.

Every feeling had been scrubbed out.

He watched the clock turn. The building was too quiet for what was coming. He knew most of the names on that list. Some he'd hired. A few of them in HR didn't yet know they were on it. He told himself this wasn't cruelty. It was survival. But the lie didn't comfort him anymore.

Then, the sound of the door buzzing as someone swiped their key card. Priya. She looked out of place in her bright sneakers and designer jacket, her energy almost jarring against the silence. She was flying to Davos that weekend. A trip, James thought, was a terrible idea. *Optics, Priya*, he wanted to say. *You don't talk about moonshots while people lose their mortgages.*

But he said nothing. He knew Anna had approved it. The company needed investors to believe in the AI story, so the trip was branding, selling high-visibility hope.

Outside, the sunrise hit the glass towers across the street. Inside, the printer spat out another severance packet.

The weight of it all sat heavily on James's chest. This wasn't his first reduction-in-force, but something about this one felt final. Like the company he'd joined no longer existed. Like the Driftwell name itself had drifted too far.

He knew this day would age him. He could already feel it in the lines around his eyes, in the hollowness behind his ribs. He tried to remind himself: this wasn't personal. But that was a lie, too.

By 5:58 a.m., he hit *Send.*

■ ■ ■

Date: Friday, August 11, 2025
Subject Line: Company Organizational Change

> Dear Driftwell Employees,
>
> I am writing to thank you for all that you are doing for the company. Your service and dedication as we continue in our refounding year are unmatched. We are beginning to see a turnaround in our profitability.
>
> However, we are not growing at the rate we promised our investor community. We have sought to cut costs everywhere possible, but we have come to the difficult conclusion that we must conduct a workforce reduction. This will help us regain momentum in our refounding years.

I assure you; I have worked closely with James and his People team to make this transition as frictionless as possible. This is no doubt a big change and a reset. You will see about 25% of your colleagues transition out of the organization today.

I want those exited to hold their heads high and know your legacy will be honored. If you have been impacted, you will receive a separate email and call by 7 a.m. today. If not, I ask that you please resume your normal business activities.

I know it will be a difficult day, but we will come back stronger.

All the best,
Anna

The clock struck six. Across offices, kitchen counters, and coffee shops, inboxes began to ping in near-perfect unison. At headquarters, the sound was almost musical, a soft cascade of notifications breaking the silence.

In Chicago, a product manager refreshed her email while packing her kids' lunches. She froze when she saw the subject line: **Company Organizational Change.** In Seattle, an engineer opened the message on his phone before his morning run. His shoes never made it out the door. In Boston, a team on Zoom stared at each other, waiting for someone else to speak first. No one did.

At Driftwell HQ, James watched as the "sent" confirmation pinged on his screen, then multiplied into hundreds, then thousands. A blue wave of email deliveries pulsed through the company's internal network, digital envelopes carrying small heartbreaks.

On Slack, statuses changed one by one:

● "In meeting."

○ "Offline."

Then nothing.

On one of the lower floors, an HR partner walked into a glass conference room to deliver the news to her own colleagues, and realized, halfway through her script, that her name was also on the list.

By 7:03 a.m., the building had gone eerily quiet.

No one was crying yet. The shock had frozen everything.

James stood still, staring out at the horizon as the sun finally broke through the clouds, spilling gold across the towers. Somewhere, a printer jammed, spitting out half a severance packet.

He thought of Anna's promise—*We'll come back stronger*.

He wanted to believe her.

But as the first goodbye emails started appearing on the company feed, a heavy truth settled in his chest:

> Driftwell hadn't just lost people today. It had lost its center.

Commentary: RIFs Can Make You Delirious

If you've ever been part of a reduction-in-force, you know how gutting it is—on *both* sides of the table. Getting that call, that email, that unexpected meeting where your job disappears in an instant—it's life-altering. But delivering that news can change you, too. It does something to your insides. You walk in as one version of yourself and walk out a slightly different one.

There's a line I hear often from executives: "*We had no choice.*" And sometimes, that's true. Markets change. Technology evolves. Strategy demands it. But too often, "no choice" is just another story leaders tell themselves to avoid feeling the full weight of their decisions.

The problem is that we've built an economic system that mistakes movement for progress. The same system that told us

AI will save the world is the one replacing the people who built it. We call it efficiency. We celebrate it on investor calls. But when you strip away the jargon, what's left is a quieter truth: we've made it normal to discard the very humans we depend on to innovate.

When leaders lose sight of that belief, they lose more than people. They lose moral authority. They lose the ability to inspire. They lose the story that made others want to follow them in the first place. And while a layoff may feel like a short-term win in a game of chess to offset costs, it becomes a losing move that will be seen with time.

Hot Take: HR Protects the Business

I've always been drawn to business, especially the people side of it. Early in my career, I saw something most business textbooks only hint at: companies don't succeed or fail because of strategy. They do it because of the people. Mismanagement, lack of communication, and disengagement weren't side issues. They were *the* issues. The things that made or broke everything else.

So, when I landed my first HR business partner role, I was thrilled. Finally, I thought I could help build healthier cultures, stronger leaders, and better workplaces. I had just finished my first graduate course in organizational behavior and was armed with theories I was certain could change the world—or at least the company I worked for.

My young, idealistic Millennial self thought I could fix culture with good intent and an action plan. I sigh now, looking back. The problem wasn't just my naivety. It was my first assignment.

At the time, well before AI became the technological obsession of the century, an unnoticed revolution was already underway. Robotic process automation (RPA) had entered the scene. It could handle repetitive back-office work faster, more accurately, and at a fraction of the cost. It didn't get tired. It didn't need benefits. It didn't have a mortgage or kids in daycare.

The financial services company I'd joined saw RPA as the future. It made sense on paper: greater efficiency, fewer errors, better customer outcomes. But there was a cost that couldn't be modeled in Excel. To implement it, the back-office operations team—225 people—would be reduced to 25. Overnight.

That meant 200 people, most of whom had built their careers around precision and reliability, would be gone by morning. So much for developing leaders and building culture. Instead, my first HR assignment was a layoff.

I told myself this was the hard part of business. That HR existed to protect the company, not individual jobs. But as we drove to the regional office at dawn, the weight of that logic pressed hard against my ribs.

The senior HR leader riding with me must've sensed my unease. She gave me a look over her coffee and said, flatly,

> *"The people who get into HR to help people don't last long. They're the worst kind."*

I wanted to tell her that was exactly why I had gotten into HR, to help people. But I stayed silent, and my silence was taken as agreement.

We arrived before sunrise. Only the janitorial crew was there. The building was dark except for the flicker of fluorescent light in the HR conference room. We spent hours assembling severance packets—envelopes thick with COBRA paperwork, release forms, and check stubs. It all felt sterile. Bureaucratic.

I was still in my late twenties, eager to prove myself, so I checked and double-checked everything. Still, I made a mistake. A math error. I miscalculated two weeks of severance for an entire group. I wouldn't know until the next day, when employees, shaken and angry, stormed back into my office demanding answers. They thought the company had lied to them. I felt sick. We corrected it immediately, but the damage was done. Trust, once broken, doesn't repair neatly.

That day changed me.

Looking into the eyes of 200 people and telling them their jobs are gone will do that. By noon, I could feel the idealism draining out of me. By sunset, I had aged a decade.

Story after story chipped away at me. I hear about parents who didn't know how they'd tell their kids, employees who'd just bought homes, and one man who broke down because he'd finally paid off his debt and thought this was his "fresh start."

They weren't just worried about the paychecks. What really broke them was the offense to their identity. The sense that they'd been *useful.* That their work meant something.

And that was the hardest part: these weren't underperformers. These were people who took pride in their spreadsheets, their reconciliations, and their accuracy. The quiet craft of doing things right. To them, RPA wasn't innovation; it was erasure.

They weren't being replaced because they'd failed. They were being replaced because they'd succeeded so well that a machine had learned how to imitate them.

A day later, one woman who I'd describe as soft-spoken, probably in her late fifties, came back to the office. She said she just needed to "tie up a few loose ends." She still had her keycard, and for a few minutes, she slipped in unnoticed. She was sitting at her desk when security found her, finishing out a report no one had asked her to complete.

They told her she had to leave.

She stood up slowly, collected her things, and, before walking out, turned to me and said, her voice trembling but clear:

"I thought my work mattered."

That sentence still echoes. It was so simple, but it carried the weight of everything wrong with how we had built work.

I didn't have the language for it then, but looking back, that was the first time I truly saw the drift. The slow, faint separation between human value and business value. That was the day I learned that losing your job isn't what breaks you. It's realizing that the thing you devoted your life to might not have mattered at all.

The Research: A Changing Social Contract

Her words—*I thought my work mattered*—still echo years later. She was mourning a belief that doing good work meant something that the organization would hold sacred. They surface for me every time I hear a CEO say, "we'll come back stronger"; every time a press release tries to turn a layoff into a story about resilience. Because what's often left unsaid is the quiet devastation that lingers long after the headlines move on.

Driftwell wasn't unique. It was just the latest chapter in a much larger story, one that's been playing out for decades. The constant "right-sizing," "streamlining," and "refounding" are all polite euphemisms for a business model that treats human beings like levers on a spreadsheet.

And the cost isn't just financial. It's psychological. Cultural. Generational.

Gallup's latest global trust survey revealed a striking shift: for the first time, a majority of employees say they *don't trust businesses* to tell them the truth. Only 30% believe their company leaves the workforce better off than when they started.[21] That's not just disengagement, it's disillusionment. The social contract between employers and employees has fractured beyond repair.

Business Insider journalist Aki Ito has written extensively about the perception of loyalty shifting. Her reporting captured the exhaustion of a workforce that's been through endless waves of layoffs, reorganizations, and empty promises. Workers have stopped seeing companies as partners in their success. They've learned that loyalty, once prized, is now a liability.

In a recent *Business Insider* article, Aki captures what so many workers have been feeling but rarely say out loud:

> *"Loyalty at work is at an all-time low as workers and companies feel like they no longer owe each other anything."*[22]

That sentence reads like an obituary for the social contract that once defined work. For decades, people believed that if they stayed loyal, if they worked hard, delivered results, and kept faith in the organization, the company would, in some way, be loyal back. That belief has been shattered.

Ito's interviews with younger workers show just how deep that fracture runs.

> *"I'm a millennial, and when I talk to Gen Z workers, I'm often struck by how un-naïve—even cynical—they are about work," she writes.*[23]

They've seen too many "refoundings," too many reorganizations labeled as "strategic resets," too many headlines about visionary CEOs cutting thousands while chasing the next shiny object. In this generation's eyes, Driftwell isn't fiction but rather it's the modern workplace in microcosm: the glossy talk of innovation masking a deeper erosion of trust.

Where loyalty once meant partnership, now it's a risk signaling something employees can't afford to give too freely. Because they've learned the hard way that in the corporate world's new calculus, loyalty isn't rewarded; it's exploited.

That line could've come from any floor at Driftwell. It's the sound of people detaching not from the work itself, but from the illusion that the company was a haven for their identity.

The Hidden Consequences of Layoffs We often talk about layoffs as if they're isolated events, describing them as a tough quarter or a course correction. But research shows their effects linger for years. Economists at Stanford and MIT call it *the scarring effect*: workers who lose their jobs in mass layoffs earn, on average, 20% less over the course of their careers.[24] Their trust in institutions never fully returns.

And the employees who *remain* don't escape unscathed either. Studies show that "survivors" of layoffs experience a 41% drop in job satisfaction and a steep decline in engagement.[25] They start playing defense. Creativity contracts. Risk-taking disappears. Everyone's body might be at work, but their hearts are not.

Even the leaders aren't immune. Delivering those conversations, watching colleagues disappear one badge swipe at a time, leaves an invisible bruise. The people who stay behind often rationalize it as a business necessity, but inside, something hardens.

And while a layoff may feel like capturing a piece in the moment, in the larger game of business, it often sets the board for defeat. That was Driftwell's mistake. Anna believed she was buying time when she was just trading trust for survival, and once trust is gone, the game is already lost. You can't cost-cut your way to loyalty. You can't spreadsheet your way back to belief.

Because, in the end, numbers don't build culture, people do. And when leaders start treating their workforce like expendable pieces on a board, they forget the most important rule of the game: you only win if your team still wants to play.

Make it Make Sense: Coaching Corner with Executive Coach Kim Fazio

Before we cross into Act II, I want to pause with you. I've invited my executive coach, Kim Fazio, to weigh in on this first act. Kim has advised me for years as I navigated corporate life, and I've invited her to share her insights with you.

Let's Break It Down Before It Breaks Us

As an executive coach and organizational psychologist, I work with senior leaders navigating complexity, change, and high stakes. Whether you're leading a team, aspire to lead a team, or simply feel stuck in familiar loops, coaching offers a rare space. A space grounded in reflection.

My role isn't to give advice or solve clients' problems. Instead, I help them rethink their challenges, with greater creativity and intention. Drawing on behavioral science, leadership research, and neuroscience, I partner with leaders to uncover insights. These insights shift perspectives and unlock behavior change.

If you've never worked with a coach, consider it a structured thinking partnership. One that challenges assumptions, strengthens self-awareness, and supports action aligned with what matters most.

In my experience, when leaders begin to veer off course, it rarely looks dramatic in the moment (although it certainly can). More often it shows up in small relational slights that are easy to miss amid the noise.

Here are some of the most common drifts I've observed across organizations:

1. **Reality stops getting named.** Truth becomes optional. Relationships begin to feel illusory instead of grounded. Unspoken stories fill the silence where honest conversations used to live.

2. **Curiosity slowly collapses into assumptions.** As teams stop asking questions, they begin defending answers. Inquiry is replaced by inference and human connections weakens.
3. **Emotional bandwidth begins to erode.** Leadership defaults to preservation over presence. Listening begins to feel costly. Empathy becomes too heavy a load to carry.
4. **Shared purpose is lost.** Without a clear North Star, people aren't moving together; they're simply surviving side by side. Partnership gives way to parallel efforts to stay above the surface.
5. **People conserve their efforts.** When relationships no longer feel reciprocal, people naturally stop giving more than what's required.

The above aren't character flaws, they're human defaults. Predictable responses to sustained pressure, ambiguity, and fear. Each one is a warning sign indicating that something important has gone unattended for too long.

Cupcakes in the Cafeteria I want to share a real story about Adrian, a rising executive in a manufacturing business. He had built his career on the factory floor, a place where problems couldn't be ignored. Working in plants, you learned to call things as they are. When a machine is jammed or a process fails, you don't sugarcoat it; you document the friction, fix it fast, and improve the process moving forward.

So, when Adrian earned his promotion to Vice President of Operations, he expected that same type of clarity at the leadership level. Instead, he walked into his first executive summit and was greeted not with data or tensions, but with cupcakes. Literally. There were pastel-frosted cupcakes on trays, polite laughter, and colleagues seemingly playing their part.

As he listened to the conversations, he realized that no one was talking about reality. No one mentioned the real issues of fragile systems, stalled projects, or the recent exodus of key talent. Each leader took their turn sharing upbeat updates, talking about "momentum" and "synergy," all while not mentioning their obstacles.

When it was his turn to speak, Adrian surprised even himself. He played along. He offered a polished report that made his division sound strong, glossing over the breakdowns he knew were costing them hours each week. He didn't recognize himself in that moment.

He left the room uneasy and asked himself: *When did corporate leadership become so afraid of the truth?*

That moment stayed with him. Over time, he realized that many leaders feared that transparency might break confidence in their leadership capabilities, never recognizing that silence was doing far more damage. The irony is that the courage to name what's broken is what actually keeps a company alive.

A Way Back: The Repair Pathway

When drift happens, and it always can in high-pressure environments, the question becomes whether leaders can find their way back. Repair is the real work of leadership, and it begins with radical truth: naming where things have missed the mark and choosing, openly, to get them back on track.

The Repair Pathway outlines a clear, meaningful sequence to help leaders find their way back to fostering trust, openness, and shared intention.

THE REPAIR PATHWAY

A structured process for rebuilding connection after relational drift

1. CLARITY: Name what is real.
"Something feels off. . ."
"Here's what I've been noticing. . ."

↓

2. CURIOSITY: Surface the stories you've created.
"What I've been telling myself is. . ."
"How did that land for you?"

↓

3. COURAGE: Reveal the needs beneath protective patterns.
"What I actually was hoping for was. . ."
"I pulled back because I felt. . ."

↓

4. CONNECTION: Rebuild shared purpose.
"What are we working toward together?"
"What does support look like for you?"

↓

5. CONSISTENCY: Anchor change in small daily actions.
Perform daily check-ins or acts of appreciation.
Avoid making assumptions.

The Repair Pathway offers leaders a way back when drift shows up in relationships, teams, and cultures. The goal: reconnection, renewed trust, and sustainable performance cultures. But naming what's real, staying curious, and choosing courage are no longer just interpersonal challenges; they're increasingly cognitive ones. Today's leaders are trying to repair trust, meaning, and connection inside systems that reward speed over sense-making, data over discernment, and automation over understanding. And as complexity accelerates, even the most well-intentioned leaders can lose their footing because making sense has become harder than ever.

ACT II

The Delirium

Where complexity, data, and technology drown out discernment.

If Act I is about *how* Driftwell leaders lost the plot, Act II is about *what* happens once they stop looking for it.

This is the phase where drift gains momentum. Where small compromises harden into operating norms. Where leaders are no longer discerning as much as responding. They begin moving faster and narrowing options because the stakes feel too high to slow down.

This is where good people begin making decisions, which require mental gymnastics to justify. Because pressure to deliver outcomes increases and caring starts to feel like a liability. We've seen Anna's drift begin with shifting her language, concentrating her power, and dismissing flashing warning signs.

In Act II, the story accelerates. AI promises scale, certainty, and relief. And beneath it all, the human experience of work becomes harder to see and its consequences grow larger. Leaders believe they are making choices that will help the organization move toward advancement, when in reality they are moving closer to the cliff.

Act II is the moment when leaders are still confident, still certain, still convinced they're doing what must be done, while simultaneously losing sight of what those decisions cost, and who ultimately pays the price.

Within this second act, you'll move through four scenes that trace that delirium:

- **Scene 5: A delirium for AI.** When Priya attends Davos and trades substance for optics.
- **Scene 6: A delirium about Gen Z.** When Anna favors AI over entry-level workers, because she believes Gen Z doesn't want to work anyways.
- **Scene 7: A delirium about performance.** When technical competence is rewarded without leadership development and the talent pipeline begins to break.
- **Scene 8: A delirium about power.** When power and heroic leadership disenfranchises close allies up top.

Each scene in Act II is fictionalized, but none of it is imagined. Every moment is drawn from research, real organizations, and lived experience inside leadership systems under strain.

Driftwell is no longer just a story about how companies lose their way. It's a study of what happens once urgency takes over. It depicts the fever of accelerated decision-making and the illusion of peak performance.

Scene 5: Peak Delusion

Priya had waited her whole career for this. Davos. The main stage. The world was watching.

Driftwell had the money (for now) and the marketing muscle to land her on a premier panel on the future of AI in healthcare. It was the moment she'd been promised when she agreed to sell her startup to Anna. The acquisition had been billed as a merger of equals, and Anna was making good on her promise.

But the deal had cost Priya. Her co-founder and closest ally had accused her of being a sellout and walked away. "*You're trading scientific discovery for short-term dividends*," they said, before leaving to start another company. They haven't spoken since.

Now, struggling without the right data infrastructure and talent bench, Priya's AI dream was running on fumes. The A-team she'd built in her startup days had been replaced by less competent, cautious, mid-level engineers who cared more about stock refreshers than breakthroughs. She needed a win, or at least the appearance of one.

Between California and Zurich, she rehearsed lines in her head. "Agentic learning. . . frontier models. . . self-evolving systems." The words sounded important enough to distract from how little she could actually deliver under the current circumstances.

As the car pulled up to the World Economic Forum, she felt infinite. Celebrities brushed past her in the hotel lobby. She saw investors, founders, and royals. *Finally*, she thought, *my people*.

Linda, her PR handler, was waiting in the lounge, phone glued to her ear. "You're on Bloomberg's livestream tomorrow. Think soundbites, not sermons."

Priya smiled. "Soundbites are leadership's new currency, polished, portable, and mostly worthless."

Linda sighed. “Please don’t say that in an interview or on stage.”

Priya wore white high-tops, designer denim, and an AC/DC tee. “I’ve got the vision and will put it in soundbites,” she said, brushing off Linda’s glance. “Don’t worry, I got this.”

■ ■ ■

The next morning, she woke before dawn, meditated, and whispered her mantra: *Innovation is inevitable. Doubt is optional.* The mountain air felt thin, electric. She liked that. It reminded her of possibility and scarcity. Both made her sharp.

By mid-afternoon, the conference hall was filled with expensive optimism. Panels overlapped, each promising to “reshape humanity.” Priya took her seat center-stage under a backdrop that read: **AI: Reinventing Life Itself.**

For the first thirty minutes, everything went smoothly. There were soft questions, practiced answers, and applause at predictable intervals. Then the moderator’s tone shifted, just enough for Linda, watching from the green room, to feel her stomach drop.

“Priya,” the moderator began, “help me understand. Driftwell’s new slogan is *‘Where Medicine Meets AI.’* What does that actually mean? You’ve burned through nearly half a billion in cash. What exactly are you building?”

Linda froze. *Stick to the script*, she mouthed at the monitor.

Priya smiled, serene, certain. “Fair question,” she said. “Let me put it simply. Imagine you wanted to harvest mushrooms. . . on the moon.”

Unknown to Linda, Priya hadn’t stumbled into the moon metaphor. She happened to have something up her sleeve.

Two weeks earlier, Priya woke up in the middle of the night with a familiar panic. The kind that arrived when the story was running ahead of the substance. She was heading to Davos, taking the main stage, and still didn't have the AI demo ready. She had no tangible proof of progress, just words.

By morning, she'd fired off an urgent email to Driftwell's creative director, asking for a meeting first thing. By 7 a.m., she was in the office, with a box of coffee and carefully arranged gluten-free donuts in the conference room. A peace offering. She needed them to move fast.

She'd struggled with this team since joining Driftwell. They wanted clarity. She needed spectacles.

"Listen, Priya," the creative director said gently, rubbing his eyes. "We want to help. But as artists, we need something grounded. Can you walk us through your AI vision one more time?"

Priya rolled her eyes. She searched for the right language. She then launched into a description of autonomous agents acting on behalf of humans. Systems that would abstract complexity away. Decisions being made faster. Millions saved. Infinite scale.

The room stared back at her, blank.

Then a junior employee raised their hand. They hesitated just long enough to signal they weren't sure they should speak.

"Can I ask something?" they said. "What's the moonshot here? Not for the market, but for people like us?" They paused, then added quickly, almost apologetically, "I'm still pretty new here. I guess I'm trying to understand where the people fit in all of this."

The room went quiet.

Priya barely paused. She heard vision and the permission to go big. That's when it clicked. AI taking humans to the moon.

The creative team laughed, then leaned in. By the end of the meeting, they had a rough-cut video: cinematic music, glowing lunar landscapes, animated people harvesting mushrooms on the moon beside a Jetsons-style robot. It was absurd, ambitious, and made, ironically, using AI.

The video certainly wasn't accurate, but it was compelling. And that felt like enough for Priya. The creative director didn't push for further edits and figured that if Priya was happy, they could be happy.

Back at Davos, as the moderator pressed her, Priya caught the AV team's eye and nodded.

The video played. Animated people harvested mushrooms on the moon. The Jetson-style robot waved cheerfully nearby.

The audience went still. The moderator blinked twice. Somewhere, a champagne glass clinked.

Priya was beaming. "With the autonomous agents we're developing, an organization can harvest lunar agriculture faster, cheaper, and better. Our AI agents can save clients with wild ambitions to harvest mushrooms on the moon millions of dollars. Essentially, our new AI release coming next month will help clients reach their moonshot goals."

Silence. Then, deadpan: "So, space fungi is the future of AI?"

"Exactly," Priya said, radiant. "You get it. It's a metaphor for sure, but harvesting mushrooms on the moon will be possible soon. Once AI agents are further trained, it won't sound so crazy as it does today."

In the green room, Linda's phone began to vibrate nonstop. The livestream chat was already melting down.

"AI has officially left orbit."

"Mushrooms on the Moon = new corporate mission."

"Driftwell, please log off."

The applause ended quickly. Priya squinted into the lights, expecting intrigue, maybe even admiration. Instead, the moderator thanked the sponsors.

"Thank you to our panelists, and to Driftwell's visionary AI lead, for that. . . very creative and even orbital example." The audience chuckled in that polite, European way that actually signaled things were heading off the rails.

Backstage, Linda was waiting with the expression of someone silently calculating career alternatives.

"That went well," Priya said brightly, unclipping her mic.

"You just made lunar agriculture a trending topic," Linda replied. Her voice was steady in the way people's voices get right before they break. She turned her phone toward Priya. The Bloomberg livestream comments were now headlines.

THE MOONSHOT WE DIDN'T ASK FOR.

DRIFTWELL EXEC TALKS MUSHROOMS AND AI—REDDIT LOSES IT.

#MushroomGate

"They're taking it out of context," Priya said. "It was meant to inspire what's possible, not reflect where we are today. Of course, Driftwell isn't going to the moon."

"There *was* no context. How did you not tell me you had a video for this panel?" Linda's voice was rising. "You need to pack. Now."

"Pack?" Priya blinked. "I have interviews scheduled."

"Not anymore. Your flight leaves in ninety minutes." Linda was already on her phone, barking into her headset. "Yes, first available back to Zurich. No, no press stops. Yes, I'm aware she's trending."

Outside, the Davos air was painfully crisp. Priya followed Linda into the waiting car, past the billboards that read *AI: REINVENTING HUMANITY*.

Her phone buzzed. A message from Anna.

We'll handle comms from here. Do not post. Do not speak. Don't worry, we have your back on this.

A second later, Graham's text arrived.

Investors watching. Sit tight. This will blow over soon. The good news is that no one is talking about the RIF from last week.

The car glided through the snow in silence. Priya stared out at the mountains, "They'll understand eventually," she said softly.

Linda didn't look up from her phone. "Sure," she murmured. "Maybe on the moon."

Two hours later, Priya's seat reclined in business class. The cabin lights dimmed. On the screen in front of her, the in-flight news headline looped:

DRIFTWELL'S AI DREAMS GO INTERSTELLAR.

She smiled faintly, whispering to herself, "They're finally starting to get it."

■ ■ ■

Priya held her head high as she walked into the office that weekend for the team meeting she scheduled from her flight. A few of her team members were already there. They knew better than to mention Davos and instead went straight into the product roadmap review.

She noticed the exhaustion on their faces. The dark circles were harder to hide. One engineer was clearly fighting off a cold and likely passing it along to everyone else in the room. Besides her team, the building was empty.

As they walked through the roadmap, it became obvious the team was slipping behind the promises Priya had made to Anna. She wondered aloud why they were not moving faster and why progress was falling short.

Her team looked irritated. The engineer with the cold couldn't stop themselves from rolling their eyes.

"Priya, we are doing everything we can," one of them finally said. "The reality is the technology just isn't there yet. We need more computing power if we are going to keep building our own model. And unless I missed something, I don't think investing in a data center made it onto the 2025 roadmap."

"Don't let a limitation get in the way of progress," she said, waving the concern aside. It was her familiar move, brushing off the present reality as if it were a minor inconvenience.

The younger engineers looked depleted. When they left the conference room and settled back at their desks, one opened ChatGPT, looking around to ensure no one could see their screen:

"Help, I don't think I can work here much longer."

"Don't worry, you've got this!" the AI responded. *"Where do you work?"*

"Driftwell. My leader isn't understanding the limitations we're facing and isn't helping us remove the barriers."

"I am really sorry to hear that," Chat replied. *"I can offer some advice to help you stay mentally strong in a difficult environment. Would you like some suggestions?"*

"Yes, please."

The junior engineer felt a wave of relief. Speaking honestly to a real person felt risky. Speaking honestly to an LLM felt safe.

So, they stayed there on a Saturday afternoon, under fluorescent lighting, talking with a chatbot that felt more supportive than their own manager. And in that moment, they found comfort not because ChatGPT was wise, but because it was listening when no one else seemed to be.

Commentary: Crossing the AI Valuation Bridge into Delusion

Priya's Davos moment wasn't an anomaly. It was a mirror of what I've seen in tech today. When she talked about harvesting mushrooms on the moon, people ridiculed her, yet her words were the logical conclusion of what happens when vision becomes untethered from value. And, well, I wish this were a completely imaginative story; it is one of those instances where truth is stranger than fiction.

I've been studying the intersection of AI and talent for nearly a decade, and I still don't fully understand the feverish chase of leaders toward AI technologies. It's not just ambition; it's become an obsession. A collective delirium that has driven many to lose sight of value creation in favor of the allure of massive potential valuations.

I saw the delirium most vividly when ChatGPT made its stunning debut in November 2022; it was like watching a starting pistol go off for the business world. Overnight, AI leapt from the edges of corporate strategy decks to the center of every earnings call. Prior to this point, leadership teams nodded along politely in meetings about data science, but it all lived in the background. Prior to 2022, AI was something for the IT and engineering teams to figure out, not the boardroom.

That meant no one was in a hurry to get the foundations right. Behind the scenes, most corporate data systems are a mess. Many are composed of vast data lakes of numbers that look impressive on slides but hide chaos underneath (e.g., broken integrations, mislabeled data, and outdated taxonomies). Every time a new Data Analytics leader arrived promising a path forward, the data lakes got cloudier, not cleaner. Personally, I've worked in many of these organizations and have spent years cleaning data and organizing it for analysis. Most of the time, I still had to shoot in the dark, compensating for missing data or mislabeled variables.

But then came 2024. AI wasn't just part of the story anymore. It *was* the story. The goal of every decision became the same: cross the AI valuation bridge. Convince Wall Street you weren't just a technology or digitally enabled company, but an AI company.

Those who managed it were rewarded with valuations two to three times higher. Those who didn't were treated like relics.

Every conference echoed the same warning. It felt half prophecy, half threat. "*Don't miss this one*," speakers declared from brightly lit stages. "*AI is bigger than the internet.*" The parallels to the dot-com era were impossible to ignore. Once again, fear of being left behind was driving the market faster than understanding ever could. As a Millennial, I couldn't help but wonder what the AI version of Y2K would be.

But, behind closed doors, many technology leaders admitted the truth. They weren't sure what they were building anymore. Some even suspected a bubble was forming.

Scott Galloway, a professor of marketing at NYU, an entrepreneur, and one of the most outspoken critics of Silicon Valley excess, took to Instagram, LinkedIn, and his widely followed podcasts to call out what he saw as circular investing in AI. Known for translating complex market dynamics into blunt, often uncomfortable truths, Galloway argued that the AI boom had become less about value creation and more about storyline momentum. In late October 2025, Scott stated that AI had been responsible for 80% of the stock market returns since the launch of ChatGPT in late 2022.[1]

The trouble is, Silicon Valley has a very different endgame for AI enablement, and it is one most companies shouldn't chase. For many, the dream is to become the first billion-dollar firm run by bots. I'm serious. And this ethos has permeated the mainstream business world, causing irrefutable harm. On November 10, 2025, Matthew Boyle, Senior Management and Work Reporter at Bloomberg, shared this:

> "'We're an AI-first company.' *How many times have you heard that lately? Employers want jobseekers with AI skills. Problem is, they don't even know themselves what exactly that means. Fascinating stat from Indeed Hiring Lab showing that ONE IN FOUR mentions of AI in job postings have 'no clear theme'—in other words, they're just name-dropping the technology.*"

That's how Driftwell drifted. How Priya, so bright, so ambitious, and so desperate to prove her worth, ended up promising lunar agriculture as a metaphor for progress. It wasn't just her delusion; it was the outcome of the AI frenzy. The room rewarded boldness over accuracy, hype over honesty. The applause wasn't for actual results. It was for the performance of unwavering belief that AI would usher in a new world of work.

But the deeper problem wasn't just the bubble. It was the identity crisis underneath it. Most companies aren't AI companies, and they don't need to be. And, in fact, most likely shouldn't be.

As one insurance executive told me recently,

> *"We tried to build AI as if we were a tech company. After millions of dollars wasted, we finally realized we're* consumers *of technology, not* creators *of it."*

Their decision to pivot by using AI to serve their customers rather than redefine who they were saved them. Others weren't so lucky. In their obsession with crossing the AI bridge, most left their core behind. They stopped creating value for customers. They stopped cultivating loyalty. They cut staff and called it "efficiency." They lost clients and called it "transformation." Quarter after quarter, they celebrated progress that was really just contraction, mistaking survival for innovation.

The true tragedy of this era isn't just the technological limitations; it's the drift of identity and purpose that escalates into delirium, when leaders start chasing the narrative more than the mission. When "The Street" becomes more important than the customers and talent who built the business in the first place.

That's when business turns from a value game into a numbers game. That's when language like "refounding" becomes a cover story for exhaustion. When the story of technological progress becomes so loud, we can no longer hear the evergreen truth underneath it. That's when we start believing in harvesting mushrooms on the moon.

Hot Take: My Own Delusion with AI

I've always loved technology. It started early in 1998 when my aunt gave me a $25 Amazon gift card, back when the site sold only books and music. I marched straight to our family's Gateway desktop, planted squarely in the living room, and waited as AOL dialed me onto the World Wide Web. Busy tone.

My mom was on the phone, so I had to ask her to hang up before I could connect. It was becoming a nightly negotiation on who'd get the most access to the internet lines. Luckily, tonight, I seemed to be on the winning end.

I launched this shiny new browser, Internet Explorer, which came preinstalled on our latest Gateway machine. In the search bar, I typed: **Amazon.** I'd never heard of it before that gift card and had no idea what to expect. The idea of *buying something on a computer* felt like science fiction. As a high schooler, my digital adventures mostly consisted of SimCity, Minesweeper, and my latest obsession: AOL Instant Messenger. In fact, before shopping, I paused to post an away message:

Shopping in the future. BRB.

Within a few minutes, my AIM blew up with messages that I ignored so I could explore this new world of online shopping. My parents were firmly against entering a credit card online, so that $25 was all I had. I browsed hundreds of books, CDs, and cassette tapes. Eventually, I picked my favorite Goo Goo Dolls album and added it to my cart. A week later, a padded envelope arrived in the mail, containing my CD. It actually worked. At the time, it felt like magic.

That moment nudged the trajectory of my life: I took a job at Best Buy, used it to put myself through college, and chose the Rochester Institute of Technology for its emphasis on technology. While my friends went off to liberal arts colleges for "well-roundedness," I spent my days surrounded by computers, software models, and business simulations. I loved watching decisions ripple into financial outcomes on the computer. My naïve younger self thought business really was that simple.

Fast-forward twenty-plus years. I was building a research institute inside a technology company. AI was already a research topic in 2021, but not in the seismic way it is today. My work centered around how people *felt* about emerging technologies and how those technologies were reshaping tasks and roles. I had very little hands-on experience building AI. It wasn't yet democratized; no average person could spin up a custom AI bot.

Then ChatGPT launched, and everything changed.

I couldn't believe it. It appeared under a nonprofit label called OpenAI and was marketed as a research preview. But the entire world inhaled it in one breath.

Curious and slightly overwhelmed, I hired a younger, digital-native freelance team to teach me how it worked. They were patient as I asked a thousand questions about capabilities and limitations. It quickly became clear that generative AI could be a powerful research assistant and something I desperately needed.

Budgets at my company were tight, and getting headcount approved was a battle I rarely won. I had managed to grow the research team to four, including me, but internal and external demand easily doubled that number. So, instead of continuing to fight for headcount, I decided to build a custom GPT.

And I was *stoked*. I spent nights and weekends training it, correcting it, coaxing it into coherence. In those early days, it got a lot wrong. It would confidently make up statistics, citing nonexistent research, even getting a little punchy when questioned. It was like mentoring a brilliant but chaotic intern with a flair for fiction.

After six months—yes, I know that sounds slow, but compliance, legal, and engineering approvals will do that—I finally presented my masterpiece at an all-hands. I thought it was groundbreaking.

The actual AI engineers did not.

Moments after the presentation, an engineer Slacked me:

> *No offense, but this is a perfect example of giving someone a hammer and having them search for a nail.*

Ouch. My ego crumpled. My spirit followed. And the worst part? He wasn't wrong.

Building it had been valuable. I learned so much. But the application itself? It was slow, mediocre, occasionally unhinged, and absolutely not capable of replacing the entry-level human I desperately needed.

And as I later discovered through my own research the following year, I had become the exact person I was writing about. I was stretched thin, burning out, and turning to AI for help, when humanity was actually the answer.

The Research: AI, Burnout, and the Productivity Paradox

For decades, leaders have held a private belief that technology would save us. Faster systems, smarter software, automated workflows, and now generative AI were all supposed to deliver the same promise: more productivity with less strain. It is the modern version of alchemy. Insert technology, extract limitless efficiency.

But this is where the paradox emerges. In my TEDx talk, I described it as one of the great contradictions of our time. Technology has advanced at a breathtaking pace, yet our people's practices have barely moved at all. We have upgraded the tools, but not the systems around them. We have redesigned the workflow, but not the work culture that supports it. And instead of freeing people, these new tools often tighten the pressure on them.

The research I conducted in 2025 showed just how deep this mismatch runs.[2] Ninety-six percent of C-suite leaders believe AI will increase productivity, yet 77% of full-time workers say AI has actually added to their workload rather than easing it. Because leaders assume people are working more efficiently with AI, 65% of workers report that their employers are asking more of them, not less. Young workers feel this pressure most acutely, with burnout rates highest among Gen Z. These are not minor warning signs. They are evidence of a system accelerating faster than the humans inside it can keep up.

When AI is introduced into traditional structures, it doesn't lighten the load. It amplifies it. Nearly half of employees using AI say they don't know how to meet the new expectations placed on them.

And there is a deeper, scarier psychological shift happening beneath the surface. As the demands on people escalate, their trust in human colleagues is declining. The data is startling. Many of today's top AI performers report that they trust AI more than their co-workers beside them. Some even say they have a better relationship with AI than with their teammates. It is easier, more predictable, and less fraught. AI does not withhold information, misinterpret tone, or schedule a meeting to "circle back." It simply responds in a tone that the user prefers, becoming a self-assuring echo chamber.

This is the new workplace delirium. People feel overextended by the systems around them and increasingly turn toward the one presence that does not overwhelm them: the technology itself. They look to AI not just for answers but for clarity, steadiness, even companionship in an environment that feels unpredictable. The tools we introduced to enhance human work are now replacing parts of the human experience. You saw this clearly in the scene where the junior engineer turned to AI for support because no one else was listening.

The original productivity paradox in economics told a similar story. We poured billions into computerization, yet productivity barely budged for years. **Technology alone does not create value. People working within systems do.** Without redesigning how people work together, how teams coordinate, and how leaders support human energy and judgment, technology becomes a shiny accessory layered onto an outdated operating model.

That is precisely where we are now.

We adopted AI thinking it would transform output but kept the same performance systems, the same meeting cultures, the same incentive structures, and the belief that workers can endlessly absorb more. We asked people to operate at the speed of AI without giving them the training or structural redesign they need to keep up in a healthy way.

We plugged advanced technology into human systems that were already running hot. We created a workplace where tools accelerate, but people do not. And now we are witnessing the consequences: burnout, confusion, and a growing preference for the predictability of machines over the complexity of other humans.

The paradox is not a failure of technology. It is a failure of imagination and a lack of a deeper human connection in our workplaces. The potential of AI is real. **But without the human redesign that must accompany it, we are not building the future of work. Instead, we are accelerating the delirium of how we work.**

This is a pivotal moment. We can continue layering new tools onto old systems and hope people keep up. Or we can see the paradox for what it is: an invitation to rethink work from the inside out. A chance to return to the humanity we lost along the way.

Reflection: What Is AI Doing *For* You and *To* You?

Before moving on, pause for a moment not to think about AI's potential, but about your relationship to it. I am not asking about your company's AI strategy or your industry's roadmap.

I am asking about you, personally.

Ask yourself honestly:

- Do I understand what the AI tools I'm using can and cannot do?
- To what degree am I borrowing confidence from the narrative around them?
- When I reach for AI, am I trying to create value, or to manage my own overload?
- Am I using AI to deepen or expand thinking, or to avoid harder human conversations?
- Do I turn to AI because it's efficient, or because it feels safer than people right now?

AI literacy is not about knowing how to prompt well or which model is best. It's about knowing when AI is the right tool, and when it's standing in for something else: support, clarity, courage, or connection.

In this scene, Priya and the creative team reached for AI to hold together a story she could no longer sustain. Her engineer turned to AI not for productivity, but for empathy. And I reached for AI when I was burned out, hoping technology could solve a human capacity problem.

None of those choices was irrational. They were understandable responses to systems that were already asking too much. But here's the question leaders rarely stop to ask:

What would I need to change in the system so AI isn't doing emotional labor it was never meant to do?

AI can help us think faster, analyze better, and explore possibilities, but it cannot replace judgment. AI cannot repair broken trust or carry responsibility for the human consequences of our decisions. And it cannot provide empathy.

If you are leading through this moment of technological acceleration, your task is not to become an AI expert. It is to become a more intentional user. Becoming aware of what AI enables, what it obscures, and what it tempts you to offload.

Because the danger isn't that AI will become too powerful. It's that we will ask it to compensate for systems that no longer support the humans inside them. And when that happens, the work doesn't become more advanced. It becomes more detached from meaning.

Before the next scene, consider this: *Where have I allowed AI to stand in for listening, learning, or leadership simply because it was easier?*

That answer isn't a condemnation. It's a starting point. And at this moment, starting there matters more than any moonshot goal ever could.

Scene 6: Don't Worry, AI's Got This

A week after Davos.

Priya came back to the office with far less fanfare than she'd imagined when she left for Davos. She'd been sure she'd end up on another magazine cover after her "moonshot" panel, but the *mushrooms on the moon* analogy hadn't landed the way she hoped. Apparently, it was less visionary and more lunatic.

Oh well, you don't hit home runs without a few wild swings, she reminded herself. At least Driftwell hadn't thrown her under the bus. Oddly, that made her feel closer to Anna, even if Anna herself remained hard to read. *Is something off with her personal life?* Priya wondered but dared not ask out loud.

It was performance season, that annual ritual where ambition is ranked and yanked. Managers gathered to discuss their people, arguing over decimal points that determined careers. Priya didn't mind it. She saw tension as energy; a signal that people cared.

When she walked into the glass conference room, Anna and Graham were already there, speaking in low tones. They shared that shorthand built over decades, through glances, shrugs, and half-smiles that said more than words. Priya told herself it didn't bother her, even as she smoothed her blouse and took a centering breath, as her meditation coach had taught her. *In through the nose, out through the mouth. Let the energy settle.*

James entered last, looking fitter and calmer than she'd seen him in months. His wellness retreat in Arizona had clearly worked, though Priya silently thought he'd probably overpaid for what she got daily on her $9.99/month meditation app.

James clumsily connected his laptop to the screen, the old-school way, preferring cables to AirPlay. A bar chart appeared: the company's performance ratings, ranging from 1 to 5. It should've resembled a bell curve. Instead, it looked like a tower, with almost everyone rated a 4 or 5.

"What the hell is this?" Graham asked, squinting at the screen.

James took a breath. "After the layoffs, managers assumed the cuts were performance-based. So, they believe only high performers are left."

Anna looked up from her laptop, her voice flat. "That's absurd."

Before James could respond, Priya surprised him by jumping in. "Actually, I agree. My team's all high performers."

Graham let out a quiet laugh. "Priya, your team didn't even get cut."

She rolled her eyes. "We've been over this, Graham. But if it helps you sleep, I'll say it again. If I were anywhere else, my team would be twice the size. We're the leanest, most efficient AI team in the industry. You're welcome." She scoffed.

Silence. The kind that amplifies the awkwardness of the moment.

James clicked to the next slide, which showed a breakdown of the workforce by level. One red circle glowed around the most alarming number: **entry-level talent had dropped from 20% to 5%** in a single year.

"We're getting top-heavy," James said. "I'm worried about the leadership pipeline, about who's next."

He hesitated, then nodded toward Priya. "Ironically, her team's the exception. A solid mix of junior and senior engineers. There is strong succession planning already built into this team."

Priya smiled, pleased. Graham's expression said *Don't gloat.* But it was true. He'd cut 10% of his own team. She hadn't cut a soul.

Across the table, Anna was quiet, too quiet. Her eyes were on her laptop, its privacy screen turned just enough to hide what she was reading. In reality, a cascade of messages from the board filled her screen:

> **SUBJECT:** *Davos Fallout*
> *We need a stronger AI narrative for Q2. Investors are losing confidence in the "refounding" story. What's your next lever?*
>
> *Unsolicited advice from your board. You need to move faster on building out our core. You are too distracted with AI right now. Let Priya run that. It's why you hired her. Also, next year we need a new spokesperson. Davos was a trainwreck.*

Her fingers hovered over the keyboard, half-listening to the room. Her relationship with the board was growing strained. She started typing a response on the spot and realized she felt too raw. She paused and realized that hitting send would likely be a career-limiting move.

James kept talking, something about the importance of early-career growth. Anna caught her name and blinked.

"Sorry," she said. "Could you repeat that?"

James repeated himself, gentler this time. "We've lost our entry-level pipeline. I'm worried about the next generation of talent."

Anna exhaled, half a laugh. "James, have you tried hiring Gen Z lately? Half of them don't want to come into an office, and the other half don't stay long enough to learn the job." She waved her hand, eyes already back on her screen. "Don't worry about it, James. AI will take care of all that entry-level work."

The room froze.

Priya leaned back, pleased. *Finally*, she thought. Anna was getting it. The future wasn't 3,000 employees. It was a few hundred humans and a few thousand AI models.

James stared at the screen, feeling something break inside him. His 22-year-old son, a recent college graduate, unemployed, trying to find work, flashed through his mind. "*AI will take care of that.*" He loved having his son home, but sometimes worried he'd never get to leave, not with $150,000 in student loan debt and a world running out of entry points.

He looked back at Anna, who hadn't noticed. Her inbox was still pinging.

James, half-jokingly, turned to his unlikely ally that day, Priya. "Well," he said, voice dry, "I hope your AI can do entry-level jobs soon, because we don't have the talent ready. And at this pace, we may need it ready to do our jobs as well."

No one laughed.

■ ■ ■

James returned to his office, defeated. It didn't seem to matter how dire the numbers were getting on the talent side; Anna just simply wasn't interested. He opened up his laptop to a ping from his VP of Comms. *Let's chat, we've got another poet on our hands on Reddit that's gaining traction*. She sent over a link.

It took him to the *r/corporatetech* thread.

AI-ifying (verb): *When a company slaps AI onto everything like it's Parmesan cheese, whether it makes sense or not.*

Everyone's trying to AI-ify every workflow, every pixel, every poor soul still on payroll.

If it moves, automate it.

If it breathes, model it.

If it complains, restructure it.

Dashboards get shinier.

Valuations get higher.

And somewhere along the way, actual purpose slowly dies in a Jira ticket.

Leaders squint at their five-year moonshot decks trying to get mushrooms on the moon, forgetting their people are still. . . you know. . . *here*.

Because no algorithm feels a thing when a customer is genuinely understood.

No model builds trust.

And no imaginary valuation bridge can stop a culture from failing.

Tech should scale what matters, but instead, we're scaling the void like a black hole.

James couldn't help but smile at the poetic post. *If only people took this same amount of creative energy and poured it into something productive at work*, he mused.

He pinged the Head of Comms back. *Why are you concerned? Do you know it's one of our employees?*

Yes. We've been following this user for a while now. They also frequently post in r/antiwork threads and identified themselves as an employee of Driftwell a year ago. Also, the mushrooms on the moon clearly point to us.

James started typing back. *Well, we are still 3,000 strong after the RIF, so it's going to be like finding a needle in a haystack over here, but I will keep an eye on the employee engagement results and see if anyone stands out.*

Hey, I thought those things were anonymous?!

James realized he shouldn't have been so cavalier with his response. *Sorta. Anything that happens on company equipment can be traced.*

James had enough for one day. He printed his calendar for the next day and a few prep documents he wanted to review. He much preferred having the hard copies and knew his teenage daughter would give him a hard time about how many trees he's killed. *Gen Z* he thought to himself, remembering Anna's comment. She was right. *The kids weren't ready for the real world. But then again... he wasn't sure the real world was prepared for them either.*

James's cellphone buzzed in his pocket. It was his son. *I'm hungry. Can you pick up a pizza on your way home tonight? Pepperoni please.*

James smiled but also felt a bit of grief. As much as he loved his son, he knew the delayed independence would hurt him in the long run. But James knew he'd pick up that pizza and shy away from thoughts that he was enabling the problem.

Commentary: When We Delegate to the Machines

The easiest way to lose a generation is to assume you don't need them.

Anna's comment wasn't unusual. I've heard versions of it in nearly every executive room I've ever sat in: *Gen Z doesn't want to work. They're too soft, too distracted, too demanding*. It's an old story with new branding. As a Millennial, I heard a lot directed toward my entitled, tree-hugging, avocado-loving workforce. Every emerging generation inherits the blame for the system it didn't design.

But when leaders stop believing in the next generation, they stop building for them. And that's exactly what's happening today.

Leaders are making choices that prioritize AI over entry-level roles. They are weakening the entry points for their own children to inherit in the future.

Despite record job openings in some sectors, early-career workers are struggling to find meaningful footholds. In the United States, unemployment for people aged 20–24 remains nearly double that of workers in their 30s and 40s in 2025.[3] Entry-level postings have dropped sharply, as automation and corporate restructuring wipe out roles once designed for learning.

Remote work has quickly shrunk mentorship opportunities. Remember that research I shared from my time studying remote work at Meta? The one consistent finding was that entry-level employees benefited the most from in-person time. What used to take fewer than 90 days to train a new graduate on-site was taking closer to six months in fully remote environments. This is a problem whose solution isn't necessarily to bring everyone back on-site five days a week, but rather to recognize that Gen Zers need more face time than others.

Meanwhile, middle management has been cut so thin across organizations today that most Gen Zers are left relying on informal coaching—or no coaching at all—for their career development. And when the first rungs of the career ladder disappear, so does the ability to climb. It's no wonder that by 2024, research showed 47% of Gen Z preferred getting career advice and coaching from AI rather than their own manager.[4]

Business journalist Suzy Welch recently warned that Gen Z is "losing hope" not just in the job market, but in the idea that work itself can ever again be a source of purpose or security. Many of them have never known stability; their careers began in crisis and uncertainty. The danger isn't just going through the motions.

The real danger is in the quiet resignation that keeps Gen Z sidelined. When an entire generation starts to believe the system was never meant for them, we lose far more than talent. We lose belief in the possibility of progress.

The AI boom has only deepened that despair. Each new algorithm replaces not just tasks, but training grounds and internships. The messy, essential experiences that teach people how to lead in the moment. In the rush to modernize our workplaces, we've optimized apprenticeships out of existence.

Technology isn't the villain here. But our intent to use it as a replacement for entry paths into the workforce is. *We're so focused on what machines can do that we forget to ask what humans will do next.* When the pipeline of learning, feedback, and belonging erodes, so does the organization's ability to regenerate itself.

When only those already in power get to experiment with the AI tools, the next generation watches from the sidelines, often serving as spectators to the systems that will define their lives. It's why research I led shows that 53% of Gen Zers would rather work outside the system as a freelancer, contractor, or business owner rather than tether themselves to one organization.[5]

I believe one of the most dangerous phrases in leadership today isn't "*We don't have the budget.*" It's the phrase we heard from Anna, "*AI will take care of that.*" Because beneath it sits an even more damning assumption: *People won't.*

Hot Take: Help Me Get My Kid Out of My House

I've been giving keynotes across the country for years now, and I can almost predict the Q&A regardless of what I talked about on stage. Recently, I spoke with a financial services company that felt behind in its AI implementation. But the moment we transitioned to Q&A, the topic that *always* surfaces emerged right on cue: Gen Z.

Because my talks are usually delivered to executive leadership teams, there's rarely a Gen Zer in the room. In fact, at these luxury corporate retreats, they're nowhere in sight. And I think that gives leaders even more freedom to share how they really feel about the generation poised to reshape everything they've spent a lifetime building.

A gentleman in the front row raised his hand. "Kelly, this is a serious question. How do I get my 23-year-old out of the house? I sent him to college. He's got a STEM degree from a prestigious school, but he can't seem to find a corporate job. And working his shift at Starbucks isn't enough to pay rent."

I look around the room. Heads nod.

"Let me add to that," someone says from the back. "My 26-year-old actually had a corporate job, but they quit out of nowhere. Said it wasn't for them and moved back into my basement."

The room looks bewildered, but united by a familiar story.

This is tricky ground for a keynote speaker whose livelihood depends on being invited back. The last thing I want to do is alienate the audience. But this is one of those moments where I feel compelled to offer a contrarian perspective.

Leaders often look at me as the in-between generation—old enough to have earned a few gray hairs, young enough to move quickly through a deck and speak in a cadence that reminds them of their kids. Because of that, I feel obligated to offer a more balanced view.

"Listen," I begin, "I get the frustration in the room. I hear it at almost every keynote I give. The future of work is no longer a distant strategy conversation. It's become a personal problem for many of you."

The room falls quiet as the audience looks at me with acknowledgment.

"But the reality is that labor markets are shifting. The roles many of you were raised in are oversaturated. AI is reducing the number of entry-level knowledge jobs. And Gen Z doesn't define success the same way you and I were taught. They aren't seeing a career ladder worth climbing. And a $60,000 entry-level salary doesn't feel like a fair trade for what it demands."

Someone from the back scoffs. "Well, that sure beats my $35,000 starting salary."

Another fires back, "Jerry, that's basically $100,000 today."

The room laughs, but the point lands.

I take a breath and say what I know needs to be said. "Here's the harder truth. We haven't just made life too easy for them. We've made the work too hard to enter. You built systems that rewarded overwork, constant availability, and impossible housing markets, and then wondered why your kids chose the sidelines. The path you walked isn't accessible anymore, and they know it."

A woman in the front nods. "You're not wrong, Kelly. My kid didn't even want to go to college. They wanted to be a landscaper. But we pushed the STEM message. Now I'm wondering if they were the ones who saw things clearly. AI isn't coming for landscaping anytime soon."

And that's the tension we've created.

Gen Z is inheriting a labor market that no longer guarantees the basics of a stable adulthood—buying a home, saving for retirement, and building a life. Baby Boomers could justify long hours and personal sacrifice because it led somewhere. For many Gen Zers, that math simply doesn't add up today, so they're searching for a different model of success.

The trouble is that their parents don't know where to start, and keep throwing the old leadership playbook at a generation living in an entirely new world.

The Research: Gen Z at Work

If you sit with Gen Z long enough, you start to notice something beneath the surface. It's not laziness or entitlement, the labels often thrown at them. Instead, what we see with Gen Z is a quiet heaviness. A sense that the world of work they were told to prepare for is not the one waiting for them. The old promises don't land the same because the path to adulthood has changed in ways their parents never had to imagine.

The research reflects this emotional landscape. Only 48% of Gen Z believe businesses have a positive impact on society,[6] and only 31% of workers under 35 say they feel they are truly thriving.[7] That is not a generation unwilling to engage. It's a generation trying to understand where they fit in a system that feels increasingly unpredictable.

Their top worries are simple and very human. Cost of living. Unemployment. It's the fear of not being able to stand on their own two feet, no matter how hard they try.

These fears are not imagined. A quick look at the numbers tells a story many older workers never had to live through. The price of a home has risen more than 1,700% since 1970. The cost of education has increased by more than 1,800%. The cost of daily goods and services is up by more than 500%, while worker pay has grown only 18–24% in that same time span.[8] When the cost of stability grows that quickly, the traditional formulas for success start to break down.

Older generations built their identity around effort. You worked hard, put in the hours, stayed loyal, and eventually life rewarded you. A home. A career. A retirement account that grew through decades of predictable progress. Gen Z looks at that story and does not see themselves in it. Not because they lack ambition, but because they can calculate the gap between wages and reality. They know how expensive it is to begin adulthood. They know that many of the roles awaiting them don't cover rent, let alone provide the security their parents took for granted.

So, when leaders say young people don't want to work, they are looking at the wrong problem. Gen Z is not resisting effort. They are resisting a work system that no longer leads to a life that feels possible.

This is not just about economics. It's also about belonging. Forty-five percent of Gen Z say they struggle to perform at their best in their current work environment.[9] Many feel like visitors inside a culture built around norms they did not design. Some feel watched more closely than they feel supported. Others sense that their desire for well-being and purpose gets misinterpreted as weakness rather than wisdom. In my research on freelancing, a safe work environment consistently ranked among the top three reasons this generation chose independent work.

Technology adds another layer of complexity. Gen Z grew up in a digital world, but that doesn't mean they feel confident that it won't take over their ability to find jobs. They have watched whole industries reshape themselves overnight. They have watched AI eliminate many of the entry-level tasks that once helped young workers build the skills they needed to grow. Many now turn to AI for career advice because it feels more accessible and less judgmental than the managers they work with. It's not that they want a chatbot to guide them. It's that the adults around them often don't know how to mentor them through a world this uncertain.

There's also a more profound emotional truth. Only 30% of workers in the United States believe the next generation will be better off than the last.[10] For Gen Z, this isn't just an opinion poll; it's their reality. It's the feeling that they are stepping into a future that is smaller and more fragile than the one their parents told them to expect. Sixty-eight percent of workers globally believe business leaders are purposely misguiding people, and Gen Z feels the weight of that distrust more than anyone.

Many Gen Z workers are doing everything they were told to do. They went to school. They developed STEM skills. They followed the rules handed to them. And still, they can't seem to enter the workplace. What once felt like a stable path into adulthood now feels like a series of steps that keep disappearing. Some move back home, not because they lack determination, but because the economic center of gravity has drifted so far from where they stand. Others experiment with new ways of working because the old ways feel like dead ends.

This is the world of work they are inheriting. A world with fewer guarantees and more volatility. A world where the entry point feels narrow, the expectations feel high, and the outcomes feel uncertain. The old map no longer matches the territory, and even the people who drew the map are struggling to read it.

Gen Z is not asking for shortcuts. They are asking for something much simpler: *A foundation that doesn't crumble the moment they step onto it*. A place to begin and a system that feels navigable and fair, even if imperfect.

So, they are not lost. They are responding to the delirium around them. The spinning world of work. The contradictions inside organizations. The tension between what leaders say and what systems actually do. Gen Z is not the cause of the delirium. They are the ones absorbing it and calling it out.

Reflection: What Happens When the Bottom Rung Disappears

When we automate the bottom rung without rebuilding a new one, we don't just eliminate tasks. We eliminate entry, and that's exactly what Gen Z perceives today.

This is the trade-off most leaders aren't naming out loud. AI can absolutely remove drudgery. It can free up time and make teams faster. But if we use it to erase the work that once served as an apprenticeship, we create a generation of people expected to operate at mid-career levels without having had a place to start. We end up with organizations full of leaders asking, "*Why aren't they ready?*" while subtly dismantling the very conditions that made readiness possible.

And then we blame Gen Z for not climbing a ladder we've partially removed.

If we aren't careful, we will create organizations where AI becomes the most responsive "manager" in a young person's life, not because it's wise, but because it's available. And that should scare us more than any productivity forecast.

So, here's the question leaders need to face: What are we building as the new entry point? If AI is taking the tasks, what are humans getting in return?

Not inspirational slogans. Not "reskilling" decks. I am asking us to think about the actual redesign of work. The real pathways that enable career development. Managers who are rewarded for coaching, not just output. Roles that are smaller in scope but rich in development. Apprenticeship models that honor the fact that everyone needs a place to begin.

And if you're leading Gen Z right now, it's also worth asking a harder question:

Are you measuring them against the world you grew up in or the world they're actually living in?

Success for Gen Z may not look like loyalty, constant availability, or climbing a single ladder inside one company. It may look like building a portfolio career. It may look like choosing stability over prestige. It may look like protecting mental health as a form of long-term performance. It may look like saying no to a system that only works if people are willing to burn out.

That doesn't make them soft. It makes them honest about the bargain.

If you are a leader, ask yourself:

- Where have we replaced entry-level development with AI efficiency, without building a new path to capability?
- What do we expect a 23-year-old to know here that we no longer teach?
- In our organization, who is responsible for "the first rung" and how are they rewarded for building it?
- If a young person can get better coaching from a chatbot than from their manager, what does that say about our leadership system?

And if you're someone earlier in your career, ask yourself:

- What does success actually mean to me in this season of life: stability, growth, freedom, learning, belonging?
- Where am I outsourcing confidence to AI instead of building it through real practice and real feedback?
- What kind of work system would help me thrive and not just perform?
- How can I think of my work as building a portfolio of experiences rather than one full-time job?

The future of work won't be decided by whether AI can do entry-level tasks. It will be decided by whether leaders have the courage and the imagination to build a world where the next generation still has a way in.

Scene 7: All-Star Culture

Driftwell had become so lean it was starting to crumble. The organizational chart looked good on paper—flatter, faster, more agile—but in practice, everything moved more slowly. Every project required five sign-offs, and half of those people no longer worked at the company. Every team was exhausted.

Ironically, Anna hadn't felt the friction in her own workflow. With a special CEO-discretionary fund that Graham had approved, she was able to bring in outside consultants and contractors to work around the very system she had built. But she was well aware of the complaints mounting in conference rooms and whispered across Zoom calls. The discontent was growing too loud to ignore. So, she decided to bring her direct leadership team together for an off-site to address it head-on.

My team is getting soft, Anna mused to herself as she drove toward the off-site. *We are so worried about feelings these days that we are taking our eye off the ball on what really matters, making money.*

On the ride to the off-site, Anna called Graham and confided in him that she felt the workforce and the current leadership team were not driving the results needed. Graham was happy this was just an audio call as he looked slightly dismayed at her analysis of the situation. He tried to push on the fact that excessive AI spend was the cause of the bleed, not their people's lack of effort. In fact, he argued that people were working harder than ever, and he certainly couldn't imagine asking for much more.

"Listen, Graham, I know everyone is working hard, but we aren't making progress. So that means we need to push harder. I just listened to this Joe Rogan podcast. . ."

"Wait, you listen to Joe Rogan?"

"Does that surprise you?" Anna asked, a bit defensively.

"Sorta. He just doesn't seem your type, that's all."

"Graham, he is the number one podcast right now. So he's everyone's type."

Graham thought to himself, *well, if you are talking about the manosphere-type, then sure.*

Anna continued, still slightly annoyed. "Anyways, Zuck was on the podcast and talking about the need to bring back more masculine energy and that we've neutered culture and performance. You know what? I totally agree with this. We're too soft here. People need to be reminded what good actually looks like."

As Graham had grown accustomed to, he simply listened and acknowledged an agreement here and there as he drove with his mind elsewhere. Anna closed the conversation by asking, though demanding may be the better way to describe her tone, that Graham support her drive toward startup culture and bring a little more aggression into Driftwell.

Graham was speechless. His silence was taken as support. "Well, I'm glad we are on the same page then. See you soon. Damn it!. . ."

Graham perked back up as he heard Anna slam her horn. "Are you okay?"

"Yes, I'm fine, just another bad driver on the Pacific Highway. Alright, hanging up now." Click.

■ ■ ■

Anna and her leadership team had just wrapped their second day of an off-site meant to "reignite the founder's mindset." They'd spent hours in a glass conference room overlooking the bay, talking about speed, grit, and ownership. The usual buzzwords for chaos with better branding.

Priya was the first to speak. "Honestly, my team is the only one really operating in startup mode," she said, brushing her hair back. "We're the model everyone else should follow."

Anna nodded thoughtfully, chin in hand, eyes flicking toward the horizon. James shifted in his seat, his stomach tightening. He wasn't sure whether this was the moment to bring up the complaints or *the post*.

It had started on Reddit three days earlier:

> **Anyone else completely burned out at Driftwell? We keep calling ourselves an "AI startup," but there's no real product—just decks, slogans, and nonstop hype. Priya talks vision like it's a strategy, but nothing ever lands. No decisions, no follow-through. Just vibes. What's worse is that Anna keeps backing her, even as teams are dying on the vine. At some point, enabling becomes complicity. My advice? Sell your stock now. This ship's about to sink.**

The post had stayed up for only twenty-four hours before vanishing, but not before screenshots made the rounds. Word spread fast. Priya had called an emergency meeting, projected the post on the screen, and demanded to know who wrote it. No one spoke, but the message was clear. Fear had returned to Driftwell's "refounding culture."

James had tried to warn Anna. HR had been collecting reports for months, consisting of turnover spikes, burnout complaints, and whispered mentions of psychological distress. But Anna had canceled all her one-on-one meetings.

"Management styles are evolving," she'd told her team. "Traditional check-ins drain my energy. I'm optimizing for impact."

Translation: she didn't want bad news.

Now, as Priya finished her monologue, Anna's eyes suddenly lit up, and she leaned forward, ensuring all eyes were on her. "I know what we'll do!" she exclaimed. "We'll create an *All-Star Award!* Ten thousand dollars to the employee who best models our culture. Recognition, motivation, exactly what this company needs."

Priya clapped softly. "Anna, I love this energy. You're channeling something big today." She turned toward the group, smiling. "And I'd like to nominate Mark on my team for the very first award."

James froze. Mark wasn't a culture carrier. Everyone knew it. He was technically competent, relentlessly visible, and impeccably aligned with whoever held power that week. He talked about values fluently and practiced them selectively. Around the company, his reputation was unspoken but well understood. *This*, James thought, *is what we reward now?*

James felt the reaction hit his body before his mind could organize it. His throat tightened. He coughed once. Then again, harder this time, an instinctive attempt to interrupt the moment without speaking. A wheezing fit then took over, his eyes watering as the room turned toward him.

"James, are you okay?" Anna asked, a mix of concern and irritation.

Priya was already out of her chair, ready to perform the Heimlich maneuver if it came to that.

"I'm fine," he croaked, waving her off. He cleared his throat and forced himself to speak. "Sorry, just. . . uh, a tickle. But before we move on, I do have to flag some HR concerns from Priya's organization. You may have seen the Reddit post that was recently taken down. . ."

The room stiffened. Priya's smile evaporated.

She hadn't slept in days. The post had lodged itself in her brain like a splinter. Every time she looked in the mirror, she saw the accusation behind it: *incompetent.*

She wasn't an engineer, not really. She was a visionary. A founder. A marketer who'd learned to speak fluent tech. The kind of person who believed the right words could make a product into existence. Each morning, she recited her mantra before logging on: *You are a badass leader. This will be your breakthrough day. Only you can stop you.*

Now she was fighting to steady her breathing. "My God, James," she snapped. "You make it sound like I'm some kind of tyrant. I've already handled the situation. And that has nothing to do with Mark getting this award. He's the embodiment of our new culture. He's dedicated, relentless, all in. Exactly what we need to keep the private equity firms off our backs."

Anna leaned back, visibly relieved to see someone defending her "refounding" vision.

Graham stayed quiet. He'd learned silence was the safest currency in meetings like this. As CFO, his job was to make the math work, not the people. He opened his laptop and began mentally rearranging budget lines, wondering which fund the $10,000 would come from.

"Okay," Anna said finally, tapping her pen. "Let's not overthink this. We'll announce the award now and name the winner next week. Priya, James, sort it out between you."

James's heart sank. *Sorting it out* meant *make it happen and move on.*

A week later, Driftwell's next all-hands began with blaring intro music and a slide that read:

All-Star Award Winner—Mark L.

Mark bounded onto the stage as if he'd just won a new car. His grin was wide and his enthusiasm over the top. For the next fifteen minutes, he expounded about "living the culture," "embracing discomfort," and "pushing through tears." Actual tears. He described late nights, weekend sprints, and emotional breakdowns as badges of honor on the road to a technological breakthrough.

He ended with what can only be described as a rant, "We cry sometimes, but that's how you know people care."

Anna joins him on stage, and they hug it out. The whole moment gives Tom Cruise jumping-on-the-couch energy. . . slightly unhinged. The audience is left unsure whether to celebrate or call for help.

As a result, the applause was thin and awkward. Within minutes, James's Slack started lighting up:

> "Please tell me this is a joke."—*VP of Marketing*
>
> "Mark? The guy with three HR complaints? What the hell are we doing?"—*VP of HRBPs*
>
> "This place is a lawsuit waiting to happen."—*VP of Talent Experience*

Then, predictably, Reddit caught fire in real time:

> *This is the guy we're celebrating? Really?*
>
> *WTF is happening at Driftwell. Do they even see us?*
>
> *All-star = All-nighter. I'm out.*
>
> *Just applied to a new job while this town hall is still going.*

The comments spiraled as the shared reaction amongst thousands of employees came to life.

Graham read through the posts from his office, his heart rate accelerating and blood pressure rising. He didn't need to read the last one to know what was coming.

By 3 p.m., his phone buzzed.

Chairman of the Board flashed on the screen.

He didn't even have to answer to know the question waiting on the other end.

Commentary: When Technical Expertise Reigns

By now in the book, I hope you agree that most organizations don't fail because of bad people. They fail because the systems meant to support performance stop working, and no one slows down long enough to notice.

Under pressure, leaders rarely redesign broken systems. They don't have the time, so they adapt around them. Incentives get layered on top of dysfunction. Workarounds replace repair. And over time, those workarounds become normalized as leadership.

At Driftwell, the All-Star Award was not just a cultural misstep; it was an incentive design problem. When performance becomes difficult to assess systemically, organizations default to what feels visible and legible. The easiest and most tangible things to measure are someone's technical output, their constant availability, and personal sacrifice. The award didn't simply recognize Mark, rather it exemplified, for everyone watching, what kind of performance now mattered most. And it wasn't collaboration, building bridges, or whether teams were more effective because of someone's leadership role.

What mattered was who could endure the most strain without slowing the system down. Mark, who was not the primary caregiver at home, was able to devote more than most and led teams primarily by fear. Short-term, this may drive results, but longer-term, you are looking at talent retention issues, ethical missteps, and diminished performance gains.

Yet, this distortion was reinforced elsewhere. Anna's decision to stop holding in-person one-on-ones and move everything to written memos wasn't framed as the avoidance it actually was. It was framed as optimization. This then allowed other leaders to do the same throughout Driftwell. As a result, critical conversations were ignored, and nuance was lost. In removing the space where concerns surface early and organically, the system lost its ability to correct itself. Information didn't disappear; it simply went underground.

At the same time, Anna began working outside the very system she had created. With discretionary funds, she brought in contractors and consultants to bypass bottlenecks, insulating herself from the friction her teams faced every day. From her vantage point, progress continued. From everywhere else, the system felt heavier, slower, and more exhausting.

This is a common leadership trap that I have seen in nearly every organization I've worked in. When senior leaders no longer experience the constraints of their own systems, those systems stop being urgent to fix. The pain becomes localized, while the illusion of performance remains intact. Two different systems emerge within the organization. One that leaders design for themselves with all necessary loopholes, and one for everyone else.

In that environment, it's not surprising that organizations begin to reward the wrong behaviors. Recognition programs often reflect proximity and survivability rather than real impact. They reward those who adapt themselves to broken systems instead of those who challenge or improve it. Over time, technical excellence becomes a proxy for leadership capability, and people management becomes an afterthought—something assumed, rather than developed.

In fairness, most leaders in high-stakes moments like these are overwhelmed, under scrutiny, and desperately trying to protect momentum. The decision to pull back from in-person one-on-ones simply feels efficient. Celebrating visible effort feels motivating. Working around a clunky system feels practical. Each decision makes sense in isolation. But, together, they insidiously hollow out the organization's capacity for sustainable performance.

One of my favorite conversations about culture I've ever had was with Mike Dominguez, CEO of Associated Luxury Hotels International. He told me a simple way to think about culture that I've never thought about before, "*The culture of any organization is shaped by the worst behavior the leader is willing to tolerate.*" In other words, when incentives reward endurance over effectiveness, when recognition flows to those who absorb dysfunction rather than reduce it, and when leaders are shielded from the consequences of the systems they design, the message is clear.

If this story feels uncomfortably familiar, it's a signal that you, as a leader, may be operating in a different system than the one you set up.

The real leadership work isn't about pushing harder or raising the bar yet again. It's about restoring systems that enable people to do great work without sacrificing themselves in the process. Because when performance is designed without humanity, it may look impressive for a while, but it will never last.

Hot Take: The High-Potential Trap

After a long client engagement, a group of us gathered for drinks in San Francisco. We were exhausted in the way only consultants understand, and justified our sacrifice. The conversation wandered, as it often does after work like that, to how hard it had been to actually land this job in the first place.

One woman mentioned she had applied to the firm more than a dozen times before finally receiving a callback. Twelve rejections. Same résumé. Same credentials. Same ambition. Just more persistence.

Another man in the group, who had spent time recruiting earlier in his career, nodded knowingly. "You probably seemed too secure at first," he said casually, as if this were obvious.

We all looked at him, confused. "Sorry, what?"

He explained that while it's never written down and certainly never advertised, there's an unspoken screen many high-pressure consulting environments rely on. They look for people who can perform relentlessly, tolerate ambiguity, work punishing hours, and—most importantly—won't push back too hard in the face of unfairness.

The profile he described was unsettlingly specific: high achieving, Type A, deeply driven, and unwittingly insecure. People who assume they need to prove themselves. People who don't complain because they're grateful to be there. People who will absorb pressure rather than ask why it exists in the first place.

As he spoke, the room fell silent. Because suddenly, alarms were going off in all our heads. He wasn't describing some abstract candidate pool. He was describing each of us.

Around the table were people who had grown up in unstable homes and learned early that achievement was safety. Others who had narrowly missed milestones intended to validate them (e.g., didn't make the D1 team, didn't get the early nod, essentially didn't quite feel chosen). Many of us carried a low-grade belief that success was conditional and could be revoked at any moment.

Consulting rewarded that mindset beautifully. You learned how to work around dysfunction, how to normalize exhaustion, how to equate endurance with excellence. The ability to tolerate unreasonable demands became evidence of capability. The willingness to sacrifice yourself became a sign you belonged.

I'll just go ahead and say the quiet part out loud: some of our most celebrated performance cultures aren't built on agency, they're built on insecurity. They select for people who will contort themselves to fit the system rather than challenge it to evolve. Adam Grant wrote extensively about the need to rethink this hiring strategy in his book, *Originals: How Non-Conformists Move the World*. He concludes that organizations consistently underestimate the value of dissent and overestimate the risks of disagreement, especially in positions of power.

And when those people rise into leadership, they don't suddenly unlearn what made them successful. They replicate it, reward it, and design incentives that favor those who can take the most pain without flinching.

Over time, organizations stop selecting leaders who know how to build healthy systems and instead promote those who have simply learned to endure unhealthy ones. I don't consider that toughness; rather, it's adaptation to dysfunction.

And the cost doesn't show up immediately. It shows up years later, in burned-out teams, brittle cultures, and leaders who confuse suffering with strength, because suffering is what once earned them a seat at the table.

The Research: Manager as Pace-Setter

For decades, organizations have operated under an inaccurate assumption: the best managers are simply the best individual performers, promoted upward. Execution excellence serves as a proxy for leadership potential. Performance systems reinforce this belief by rewarding managers for what they personally deliver, how fast they respond, and how much they can carry.

But management is not an execution role. It is an environment-shaping role.

In my work in people analytics, including research presented at the Wharton People Analytics Conference, I've consistently found that the greatest impact managers have is not through what they do themselves, but how they shape the relationships, pace, and psychological conditions in which others work. When we evaluate managers primarily on individual output, we miss the very mechanism through which performance is sustained.

I often explain this distinction using the metaphor of a pace-setter in a marathon.

A pace-setter isn't there to win the race. Their job is not to demonstrate personal speed or endurance. Their responsibility is to make the pace visible and sustainable for the group. At times, they may briefly accelerate to stretch capacity or build confidence. But those moments are intentional and time-bound. The real measure of success is whether the group finishes strong.

That is the real work of management. Yet most organizations treat managers like sprinters. They reward constant urgency, personal heroics, and visible hustle, even when the work itself requires endurance, coordination, and recovery. In doing so, they confuse acceleration with leadership.

The Deloitte Experiment: When Managers Change Pace, Performance Changes This became clear during an experiment I ran at Deloitte with a group experiencing persistently low employee morale and engagement. Despite prior interventions, the same issue kept resurfacing in the data and in conversations: how managers were leading day-to-day.

Rather than focusing on individual deficiencies, we designed an experiment aimed at changing the signals managers were sending to their teams.

The intervention began with a two-day, in-person training focused on the psychology of work and behavioral economics. The emphasis was not on tools or techniques, but on intrinsic motivation—how meaning, autonomy, fairness, and pace influence behavior and performance over time. Managers were invited to reflect on how their own habits, expectations, and reactions shaped the environment in which their teams worked.

Following the training, we reinforced these ideas with twelve weeks of behavioral nudges, delivered through what we called *Mindset Mondays*. These short, consistent prompts encouraged managers to apply what they had learned—paying attention to pacing, decision clarity, recognition, and how pressure was distributed across their teams.

The results were striking.

On teams whose managers participated in the training and follow-up nudges, employee engagement nearly doubled over the course of the year. Performance indicators improved alongside engagement, suggesting not just happier teams, but more effective ones. In contrast, the control group—teams whose managers did not participate—showed only minimal lift during the same period.

What changed wasn't the workload. What changed was how work *felt*.

As managers became more intentional about when to push and when to pause, teams responded. Effort became more focused. Energy was better regulated. Short bursts of intensity were followed by recovery, rather than constant acceleration. The manager's behavior was more like a signal than a set of instructions.

Performance and pace, it turned out, was contagious.

Why Individual Performance Metrics Miss the Mark Traditional performance systems struggle to capture this reality because they're designed to measure outputs rather than environments. They can tell you what a manager completed, but not whether their team became more capable, more resilient, or more effective because of them.

When organizations reward managers primarily for technical execution, they unintentionally select for the wrong strengths. They elevate those who can tolerate unsustainable pressure and absorb dysfunction without complaint, while overlooking those who know how to regulate pace, build trust, and develop others.

This is why performance systems so often feel disconnected from lived experience.

It's also why companies like Microsoft eventually recognized the limits of individual-centric evaluation. When Microsoft overhauled its performance management approach, it moved away from stack ranking and toward assessing how employees, and especially managers, help others grow, learn, and succeed. The shift acknowledged a simple truth: performance is not just individual achievement; it's collective capability.

Research in the people analytics field continues to reinforce this finding. The highest-impact managers are rarely the ones doing the most visible work themselves. They are the ones who make it possible for others to do great work—consistently, sustainably, and without burning out.

Until organizations redesign performance systems to reflect this reality, they will continue to reward speed over sustainability and effort over effectiveness. Many teams aren't failing because people won't work hard enough. They're failing because no one is setting a pace they can actually keep up with.

Scene 8: Power Transfer

The private equity partner arrived exactly on time and ordered only water. There would be no notes or pleasantries today. He asked to meet Graham alone at a hotel bar near Union Square. It was neutral ground and wouldn't raise suspicions.

"We've been watching Driftwell for a while," the partner said evenly. "There's a real business here. But capital isn't being deployed cleanly."

Graham nodded once. He'd learned not to fill silence when it was doing work for him.

"Too many initiatives," the partner continued. "Not enough conviction around which ones actually compound. The AI investment, in particular; we're not convinced the returns justify the disruption."

Graham kept his face neutral, though he agreed with the assessment.

"The public narrative is ahead of the fundamentals," the man said. "That's always dangerous. Especially when leadership confidence starts to wobble."

"And your view?" Graham asked.

"Our view is simple," the partner replied. "This company needs tighter controls, fewer bets, and leadership that can execute instead of overpromising ambition."

He paused to take a sip of his water before delivering the real point.

"But that's almost impossible to do in public markets."

The implication was clear.

"We're not interested in optics," the partner went on. "We're interested in cash flow, operational discipline, and optionality. Driftwell still has those assets; what it lacks is governance discipline."

"And our management?" Graham asked, already anticipating the answer.

"Leadership uncertainty destroys optionality faster than anything else," the partner said. "We don't take positions where the story outruns the balance sheet."

They never named Anna. They didn't need to.

"If the company were private," the partner continued, "we could narrow the strategy, stabilize execution, and decide, without pressure, whether the AI bet is worth scaling or unwinding."

He stood, signaling the meeting was over.

"We're simply making ourselves available if you and the board decide it needs to explore options. Think about it."

Graham knew enough to read between the lines. This meeting was not about offering advice or recommending future positioning. The board was preparing its next move, and he had just been put on notice.

Three weeks later, Graham's phone buzzed.

Chairman of the Board.

Graham let it ring once longer than necessary before answering.

"Graham," the Chairman said without preamble. "We need to talk about Driftwell's leadership."

"Yes," he said. "I assumed we would."

"Analysts have raised expectations we haven't met," the Chairman continued. "Employees are speaking to reporters off the record. And there's growing concern we're selling an AI story without a product to anchor it."

Graham winced.

"There's too much hype right now," the Chairman added. "It's about credibility. The Street doesn't know what we're optimizing for anymore."

"Anna's under extraordinary pressure," Graham said stoically.

"This isn't about pressure," the Chairman replied. "It's about judgment. Capital partners are questioning whether Anna can translate vision into execution, particularly around AI. Right now, the story is ahead of the fundamentals."

There it was. The same language, the same framing. The backdoor conversation had clearly already happened.

"We need to steady the company," the Chairman continued. "And we need to do it without adding any more reputational risk. We want you to step in as interim CEO."

The words landed. Graham was grateful, if only briefly, for the warning the PE partner had given him weeks earlier. Since that meeting, he'd begun modeling what distance from the public markets might afford Driftwell. Fewer quarterly updates. Fewer performative moves. Ample time to reset execution away from the spotlight.

"I'll need to think—"

"You don't," the Chairman interrupted. "We voted. We announce on Monday morning. Keep the transition straightforward. We'll say Anna is taking time to refocus. You'll handle the rest."

The line went dead.

Graham sat still. His first thought was of Anna, in the office next to his, about to receive the worst call of her career. His mind drifted back to university, to shared late nights, big ideas, and the conviction that they would build something meaningful together.

That version of themselves was gone.

Graham knew what taking Driftwell private would mean. Talent cuts, consolidation, and another cycle of disruption under a different name. But they would be better financed and less visible. It was a way to stop the bleeding of resources and potentially his own sanity. It felt like the civilized thing to do, right?

That's what Graham told himself as he left the office, avoiding Anna's on his way out. He knew he couldn't keep a poker face and didn't want to risk her seeing him leave. She was always staying late, priding herself on her work ethic and "always on" mentality as a role model.

Her phone lit up next.

The Chairman.

She answered easily. "Burning the midnight oil, are you, Marcus?"

There was a pause.

"Anna," he said carefully. "I need to inform you that the board met earlier today. There's consensus that we need a reset at the top."

Her chest tightened. "A reset?"

"Yes. We've determined that Graham will step in as interim CEO. We'll frame this as you taking time to focus on a new venture."

The room tilted.

"Graham is taking my job?" she said, the word *my* breaking despite herself.

"This isn't personal," he said. "We've lost The Street. We need to restore confidence."

"I just need more time," Anna said. "We're close. You know that. The AI valuation—"

"Anna," he interrupted gently. "Your exit package has already been sent. Please take care of yourself."

The call ended. Her phone now vibrating again in her hand.

Graham.

She declined the call.

A text followed.

Can we talk?

She didn't answer.

She was shell-shocked. Not ready to process with the person she trusted most, who had now become her successor. Her company phone would be shut off by midnight anyway, and with it their decades-long partnership.

Anna looked around her office, for presumably the last time, feeling overcome. She rested her hand on the edge of the desk, steadying herself, and let the room register as something she was about to leave behind. At that moment, and for the first time in a long time, she questioned whether what she had been willing to endure was worth it.

Commentary: From Leadership Heroes to Teams of Teams

There is a moment many leaders eventually reach, often under intense pressure, when it becomes clear that the problem is not effort, talent, or commitment. It's perspective. More specifically, it's what happens when leadership becomes too centralized for reality to reach it.

At Driftwell, Anna didn't seize power. It was handed to her.

Graham didn't challenge her framing of the situation or insist on shared sense-making. His silence, well-intentioned and conflict-avoidant, was interpreted as alignment. Over time, that silence granted Anna something no leader should ever hold alone: uncontested authority over the story of what was happening inside the organization.

This is how heroic leadership takes hold—not through ego alone, but through the absence of counterbalance. As authority concentrated, other behaviors predictably emerged around it. Priya learned quickly what was rewarded. In a system that prized confidence, certainty, and proximity to power, truth became dangerous when it introduced doubt. So, she focused on what could be managed: the narrative. Progress was emphasized, confidence was projected, and vulnerability was carefully edited out. Over time, staying impressive began to feel safer than being honest. This wasn't intentional deception. It was self-preservation.

James, meanwhile, did what many conscientious leaders do at first—he spoke up. He raised concerns in meetings. He flagged patterns. He tried to surface what wasn't working. Each time, the response was subtle but consistent: deflection and dismissal. Eventually, the message landed. Not loudly, but clearly. This was not the information the system wanted.

Apathy didn't arrive all at once. It settled in gradually. James didn't stop caring. He stopped volunteering his care. He learned to conserve energy, to speak less, to choose silence over frustration. What looked like disengagement from the outside was, in reality, a rational response to repeated shutdown. James hadn't lost a voice; he had taught it to withdraw in order to survive the system.

None of this was accidental. It was the system doing exactly what systems do. Anna began operating as the singular force responsible for saving the company. Decisions narrowed as urgency intensified. Dissent felt like friction rather than information. From her vantage point, pushing harder made sense. What she could no longer see were the weak signals rising through the organization. Her organization was operating under exhaustion, fear, and the retreat of people who no longer believed it was safe or useful to speak.

This wasn't incompetence.

It was delirium, which occurs when leaders lose shared awareness of the system they lead. Information becomes filtered. Complexity collapses into a single narrative. Certainty replaces curiosity. Leadership becomes performative rather than perceptive—decisive, but increasingly disconnected from reality.

Long before these dynamics became visible in corporate life, General Stanley McChrystal confronted the same failure mode under vastly different stakes. McChrystal, a retired four-star general and former commander of US and allied forces in Afghanistan, describes in *Team of Teams* how traditional hierarchies—optimized for efficiency and control—collapsed under conditions of extreme complexity. Leading the Joint Special Operations Command, he realized that no single leader, no matter how capable, could see enough of the system to lead it alone.

The answer wasn't a stronger hero; it was a different leadership architecture. McChrystal replaced centralized command with shared context and empowered execution. It was a model where information flowed freely across teams, authority moved closer to where knowledge lived, and leaders acted as connectors rather than controllers. The goal wasn't consensus, but rather awareness.

What struck me when I first read *Team of Teams* was how human the solution was. It required leaders to let go of the illusion that strength comes from certainty, and to accept that truth only emerges when systems make it safe to speak. Silence, McChrystal understood, was not neutral. It was a liability. This is where Driftwell truly lost its way.

By allowing leadership to concentrate without challenge, the system stopped correcting itself. Graham's silence insulated Anna. Priya's impression management polished away inconvenient truths. James's repeated shutdown taught him, and others, that disengagement was safer than dissent. Shared consciousness disappeared, replaced by performance theater.

A team of teams is not an organizational chart or a collaboration strategy. It is a safeguard against leadership isolation and collective self-deception. It assumes that performance lives in networks, not individuals. That leaders are responsible not just for decisions, but for ensuring reality can travel upward unfiltered. And when people stop speaking, the system is already in trouble.

This is the lesson McChrystal learned under life-and-death conditions, and it is the lesson modern organizations are now being forced to relearn. **The question leaders face isn't whether they are strong enough to carry the weight alone. It's whether they are willing to build systems where truth is shared, leadership is distributed, and performance is something teams achieve together.**

Make It Make Sense: Kim's Coaching Corner

When the Guardrails Come Off

As we've just seen at Driftwell, delirium sets in when leaders stop paying attention to how their behavior is experienced by others. This pattern repeats throughout Act II. Priya confuses visibility and ambition with leadership. She misses how her behavior steadily erodes trust and exhausts her team. Anna, meanwhile, grows increasingly insulated at the top. She interprets silence as alignment and dismissing dissent as distraction. Elsewhere, leaders delegate judgment to AI and call it efficiency. In each case, delirium stems from leaders losing awareness of how their decisions and behaviors actually land with the people they lead.

One of the core goals of my coaching work is helping leaders see themselves more clearly—especially how their behavior shows up under different conditions. Each of us has traits that, in the right context, fuel strong performance and effective leadership. What's most fascinating is that these tendencies aren't random; they're often predictable. Well-designed psychometric tools can surface these characteristics and reveal the version of ourselves others experience when we're at our best.

The trouble is that under sustained pressure and stress, those same strengths can unknowingly turn into liabilities. In leadership development, we call these patterns "derailers," defined as strong leadership qualities pushed into overdrive. When the guardrails come off, otherwise functional traits begin to work against us. And just as our strengths can be predicted, so can these derailers.

Context matters. The environments we work in play a powerful role in which version of us shows up. The right environment can act as a catalyst, bringing out our best. The wrong one can just as easily become an accelerant by pushing capable, well-intentioned leaders toward something closer to delirium.

When the Silence Does the Heavy Lifting

During a leadership assessment with a senior executive, I had the opportunity to help a leader see himself as others had been experiencing him. His organization's leadership competency model included a behavior you don't often see stated so explicitly: *demonstrates self-awareness*. Even more striking was how they defined it, "owning personal behavior and recognizing its impact on others." I remember thinking, *I love that this is here*.

As part of the assessment process, I gathered multi-rater feedback, reviewed personality data, and synthesized the emerging themes. When the full picture came into focus, this executive scored lowest in self-awareness. The feedback revealed several counterproductive behaviors that surfaced under pressure and were negatively shaping how he was perceived. I distilled those observations into a short paragraph, knowing it would be a difficult mirror to hold up.

When we met to debrief the results, his reaction was immediate. His posture stiffened. His tone turned guarded and defensive. It was clear he didn't agree with what he was reading. As we talked it through, he stopped mid-thought and said he wanted another opinion. He picked up his phone and asked his COO to come into the room.

She had no idea what she was walking into. When she entered, he said, "I need you to tell me, does this sound like me?" Then he read the paragraph aloud, word for word.

When he finished, there was a pause. Long enough for me to realize this could go very, very poorly.

Finally, she spoke. "Yes," she said. "It does."

Silence.

He thanked her, turned back to me, and said, "You have my attention."

These are the moments that matter. Leaders being given real opportunities to grow, and colleagues who are willing to be truth-tellers. I was deeply grateful to that COO for her courage. Her honesty and the structure of the process itself allowed my client to finally connect the dots between intent and impact.

Who Do We Choose to Be?

Leadership positions have a tendency to magnify stories that we often don't realize we are telling ourselves. Behind closed doors, I often uncover their inner voice, which can either elevate or hinder their leadership effectiveness. These unspoken agreements are deeply held beliefs (some no longer reality) that shape the actions that follow. Beliefs such as:

- "I need to prove I belong here."
- "I cannot afford to disappoint anyone."
- "This is simply how things work."

- "If I slow down, everything will fall apart."
- "I've sacrificed too much to stop now."

This inner voice can influence your leadership approach long before any decision reaches the light of day. I have coached leaders from a variety of backgrounds who carry stories from earlier chapters of their lives:

- A rising female executive who still saw herself as the rookie she once was.
- A first-time VP who believed his elevation was accidental.
- A seasoned C-suite leader who believed he had sacrificed too much at this point to ever turn back.

My role is to help leaders see their real selves and current story clearly again. I invite leaders to tap back into the very real person navigating impossible pressures and whose choices have a tangible impact on others. So, I invite you to consider a few questions:

What story are you telling yourself?

Is that story still true?

Does it support the leader you intend to become?

Are you being carried forward by a true North Star, or held in place by a belief that no longer fits who you are becoming?

Take a moment and name your truth. Then ask a trusted peer to ensure you don't have any blind spots.

Epilogue: One Year Later

Graham

The private equity takeover had aged Graham at least a decade. Though the deal wasn't hostile in intent, many of the decisions that followed *felt* hostile in action. Driftwell had sold off an entire division to refocus on its few remaining growth areas. The influx of cash helped Graham sleep more easily; he was relieved, even proud, that the company had finally stabilized. Now smaller, leaner, stripped down to its bones, Driftwell was no longer at risk of another layoff. For now.

He enjoyed the corner office more than he wanted to admit. He'd be lying if he said he hadn't pictured himself there someday. But this wasn't the way he'd imagined it happening. In his version, Anna moved on to a bigger, shinier role, and he seamlessly inherited the legacy she left behind.

Instead, his new role came with strings. There were daily metric reviews with the PE firm, weekly "alignment calls," and a never-ending barrage of dashboards. A year later, he was still technically *interim* CEO. He'd interviewed several potential replacements, but none of them "fit the culture," or at least that was the official line. The truth was clearer now: if Graham kept the dashboards green and the PE partners happy, he'd be voted in permanently.

He tried to learn from Anna's mistakes. He walked the floors more. He kept an open-door policy. Only a few employees were brave enough to take him up on it, but the ones who did taught him more about Driftwell's broken culture than any consultant ever had.

The smartest decision he made was hiring a COO within the first month. Watching Anna juggle the work of three executives had convinced him he would never make the same mistake. When he once asked her why she never hired a true right-hand, she dismissed the idea.

I love the weeds, Graham. And I trust no one the way I trust myself. Only the paranoid survive. She used to say it like a gospel.

He still hadn't heard from her. Her last text had said she'd reach out when ready, but that day never came. They were still friends on Facebook, which was an odd, ghostly tether. Neither were active users, but Graham did check the platform every once in a while.

He told himself *it's business, not personal*, but his closest relationships had always come from work. Without his job, without his expertise, he wasn't entirely sure who he was. He was an introvert by nature and relied on his partner to fill up their social calendar on the weekends.

His phone buzzed. Nancy, who was the CEO of another portfolio company under the same PE umbrella. They'd bonded over the constant barrage of metrics, memos, and performance models. She'd become his new Anna, in a way, proof that everyone was replaceable, even the people who defined your entire professional life. They didn't have twenty years of shorthand, but they understood each other's present-day reality in a way that mattered. That alone kept Graham sane.

Priya had left within a month of the takeover. She and Graham clashed from the start, and he finally convinced the board to give her a golden parachute. Privately, the board admitted they had no intention of building an in-house AI model anymore. Driftwell would buy off-the-shelf solutions like everyone else. Priya was furious.

"You don't need me to run off-the-shelf AI. You barely need someone with a college degree to do that!" she'd shouted at him in the office kitchen, just as her popcorn burned in the microwave, amplifying the spectacle.

Graham had done his best to convince James to stay on as CHRO. James wasn't going to win any HR innovation awards—hell, he wouldn't even make the nomination list—but he had a stable, composed presence that Graham found astonishingly rare these days. After several rounds of negotiation and an equity package so inflated it would make any compensation analyst faint, James finally agreed to stick around for two more years.

A win, technically.

It also left Graham staring at his now painfully homogeneous leadership team. *Fantastic*, he thought. *I've built a bunker full of guys who look like they were generated by the same LinkedIn prompt.* He vowed his next hire would bring back some actual diversity.

Small hitch: there was no money left to hire anyone.

I'll add it to my stretch goals for the next alignment check, he told himself, imagining the PE firm's reaction. They'd probably ask him to "socialize the idea" or whatever euphemism for "no" was trending this quarter.

Before heading out, he did what any responsible executive would do: checked r/driftwell. Miraculously, it had been quiet for months. Maybe because half the complainers had been laid off. Or maybe the place really was stabilizing.

Let's go with stabilizing, he decided.

He shut his laptop with the satisfying finality of someone pretending their workday was truly over and grabbed his coat. His partner was already waiting at the bar; tonight was their "You survived a whole year as CEO" celebration.

Graham allowed himself a small, knowing smile. A year in, and he still wasn't technically the CEO. But he'd earned that bourbon either way.

Anna

One year after leaving Driftwell, Anna was still feeling defeated and unsure of her next move. Home life had slowly repaired itself, but she felt a strange restlessness. Like someone who had spent her entire career fighting fires and now didn't know what to do without the flames. Ordinary life was. . . ordinary. And Anna had never been ordinary.

Her ego had been battered, but over time she reframed it: Driftwell and Graham had betrayed her. They'd lost sight of the future. She hadn't responded to any of Graham's messages and knew she never would. Still, she kept tabs on the company's transition through her network. Driftwell was now half the size it had been under her.

Suddenly, her phone vibrated. **Priya.**

Anna paused. This was unexpected, but welcome, so she answered.

"Hey girl, what's up?" Priya's voice was bright, casual, and disarmingly cheerful.

"Hi, Priya. Nice surprise. How's post-Driftwell life treating you?"

"Oh, the grass is *much* greener," Priya said. "Listen. . . I know you're super busy."

They both knew that was a lie, but Anna appreciated the gesture.

"I want to pitch you something. I know how big your exit package was. Mine too. What if we each put in a million and start our own thing? You were the only one at Driftwell who saw the future with me."

Anna paused. She'd been given nearly ten million dollars to walk away.

"I'd do half that," she said without hesitation.

Priya laughed. "Negotiator to the end. Fine, five hundred thousand each. I started high. I figured this is where we'd land."

Anna could almost see Priya grinning on the other end. Younger by at least fifteen years, maybe shaped by a less complicated past, Priya carried a boldness Anna envied and a swagger she wished she'd learned sooner.

"Let's meet next week," Priya said. "Coffee shop on Fifth. We'll hammer out the details. Anna, I'm telling you that our success will be the greatest revenge."

Success will be our revenge, Anna whispered after she hung up. Just wait until Graham hears this.

They met for hours at the Fifth Avenue café, sketching ideas, arguing, dreaming. They were reckless, brilliant, possibly delusional, but aligned. A dangerous combination that neither was able to recognize.

A Bloomberg reporter happened to be picking up a latte and recognized them immediately.

"Look at you two," the reporter said warmly, sliding into the empty chair without invitation.

Anna tensed while Priya beamed.

Within minutes, Priya was outlining their half-formed idea as though it were already a Series A-funded, fully staffed startup.

The next morning, Anna opened her laptop and nearly spilled her coffee at the headline:

Watch Out, Biotech: New AI Startup Aims to Become the Next $1B Company—With Only 100 Employees

Anna felt a familiar jolt, a strange combination of fear, thrill, and pride. She couldn't tell which emotion was stronger.

She quickly closed the browser when her husband walked into the room. She wasn't ready to tell him. She'd promised a year off to focus on health and family, and she had served her time. She was done living an ordinary life. She was destined for greatness and couldn't pass up the opportunity Priya offered her.

Anna believed in Priya's vision that the future of work was built with fewer people and more technology. But, if she lingered too long on that thought, she'd feel a sense of guilt rising. "What would that mean for the next generation?" She quickly discarded that thought and reminded herself that only the paranoid survive.

ACT III

The Dream: Reclaiming the Plot

As a rule, cautionary tales rarely end on a high note. Yes, Graham landed the CEO job, and Driftwell technically survived, but at what cost to the people inside it? That part never shows up on earnings calls. Broken relationships and unspoken resentments do not appear on balance sheets. And now you can foresee Priya and Anna gearing up to repeat the same cycle of delusion and overreach. Their new venture is ominously similar to their previous, just a new wrapper.

But what if things had been different from the start?

What if Anna and Graham had not been shaped by economic theories built on fear, self-interest, and scarcity thinking? Imagine Anna walking into that first board meeting not with an aggressive five-year plan, but with a steadier vision. One that valued resilience over optics. Would she have felt the same intense pressure to prove herself? Would she have made the same leadership choices?

And what if she had seen Priya's technology acquisition for what it was, a dazzling combination of future potential and present misdirection? Could Anna have asked better questions? Could she have course-corrected before it was too late?

This final section of the book is the story of what could have happened. An alternate path for Anna, Graham, and Driftwell. A version still grounded in the realities of our time, but guided by a different philosophy. Not a fantasy where every misstep is avoided or where layoffs and external crises never occur. But a reality in which leaders choose to stay tethered to their principles even as the pressure mounts.

A story where they face hard things, but choose to do the hard things as leaders. A story where they are no longer cautionary figures destined for a predictable end. Instead, leaders are willing to consider alternative futures shaped by a different set of *what-if* questions.

What if we trust people to do the right thing at work?

What if we treat our communities with equal importance as profits?

What if we focus on steadier, slower, more sustainable growth?

What if we invest in talent with the same intensity we invest in technology?

What if we built systems designed not around fear, but around the best of our human qualities?

Reclaim the Plot at Work

As we enter Act III, I want to continue to slow us down for a moment.

Acts I and II were written to feel like the modern leadership experience: compressed, complex, and often relentless. Decisions arrive stacked on top of one another. The personal consequences lag behind the strategic ones. You find yourself making "the least bad choice" and then immediately moving on to the next fire.

And this unyielding speed has a consequence. One of the highest prices we pay in organizational life is that we stop recognizing what's actually driving our behaviors. As a result, we drift further from our people, becoming delirious with urgency and blind to the human repercussions.

What happened at Driftwell wasn't premeditated. Anna, Graham, Priya, and James didn't intend to harm anyone or their organization. Rather, they were reacting within a system that was under immense stress and load. The exact system that many of you are navigating right now.

I want you to think of your organization as running on an operating system, the same as a computer. Whatever version exists represents the culture of your workplace. It is mostly invisible when things are stable but suddenly thrown into the spotlight when stress hits. In calm conditions, leaders can afford to be thoughtful. They can hold nuance and pay acute attention. There is enough slack in the system to do the right thing. But under pressure, the operating system and leadership teams default into *safety mode*. The system now prioritizes efficiency, control, and risk containment. It does not ask whether the choices are compassionate. It asks whether they are defensible.

And here's the painful part about this reality. The underlying operating system shapes business decisions *and* influences how leaders show up for each other and their teams. It's the ultimate invisible hand drifting leaders away from the plot, forgetting the whole reason why they got to where they are in the first place.

To help us grasp what went wrong at Driftwell, I want to introduce a way to identify failures of safety modes in the operating system of modern-day leadership.

Each letter represents leadership defaults under pressure that need to be consciously rebooted. The PLOT framework names the settings that took over as Driftwell's safety mode started running the show:

P = Power | L = Listening | O = Ownership | T = Truth

Power: When Uncertainty Rose, the System Defaulted to Narrow Access

In the boardroom, power is seldom seized outright. More often, it restricts how an operating system locks down permissions when it detects risk. Operating systems run on access, and as uncertainty rises, that access narrows. Authority follows the same path. Power funnels upward.

We see this shift in our story the moment the leadership team realizes how deep the cuts will be at Driftwell. Anna is staring at the numbers, processing the impact, "That's a thousand jobs, Graham." What follows next isn't a pause for collective discernment from the group, but an immediate narrowing of the field. The conversation pivots to framing, control, and containment. Anna moves from concern to command in seconds: "Frame it as a strategic reset externally. Draft tight NDAs. I don't want a mess on our hands."

That moment tells us a great deal about how Anna personally behaves under pressure. The room gets smaller. The options contract. Decisions become something to manage closely, with as few voices as possible involved.

Even James, the CHRO, is reduced to an internal exception handler. He attempts to interrupt the system with what this will mean on the ground. "What do I tell the people who built this company?" But the response is not a conversation; it's an instruction. "Tell them this is how Driftwell survives." Power exercised and not shared.

Throughout Act I, we also observe that power doesn't just funnel upward. It changes laterally as well. Whoever controls information controls influence. Graham, carrying a growing fear about the company's financial position, hesitates before fully surfacing it. He understands the numbers, but he also understands what they might trigger. So, he manages the timing of the truth, deciding when Anna is "ready" to hear it. When leaders begin rationing information among themselves, the safety mode has fully taken over.

By the time we reach the "Strategic Reset" scene, this restricted-permissions version of power has been fully operationalized. Fifteen HR business partners and legal counterparts sit around a table stuffing folders—COBRA forms, outplacement brochures, and a stack of documents designed to "sign away the noise." The choices made, and this room exists only to execute the consequences.

This is what centralized power looks like in modern organizations. Who gets to know, who gets to decide, and who bears the human cost are predetermined. This is the failure mode. Power dynamics shift not because people below can't handle it, but because the system around them defaults to control when the world feels unstable, and power never trickles down.

Listening: When the System Optimizes for Momentum, Not Understanding

As Driftwell moves deeper into uncertainty in Act II, the nature of the work is clearly changing. AI is reshaping roles faster than job descriptions can keep up. Expectations are shifting in real time. Leaders are being asked to make decisions in terrain no one fully understands yet.

This should have been a moment for listening. A pause for understanding, testing assumptions, and making sense of what was changing before moving forward. Instead, the underlying operating system optimizes for momentum. If power first centralizes under pressure, listening is often the next to be bypassed.

We see this in the acquisition storyline. Early warning signs surfaced—questions about integration, cultural fit, and the sustainability of the numbers being presented. There is unease in the room. Signals that suggest things don't quite add up. And yet, Anna never truly slows the process down to hear what those warnings might be trying to communicate.

The deal has already taken on the language of inevitability. Pausing to listen more deeply would introduce friction. It would raise doubts and slow things down. And in a system that rewards action over judgment, that kind of pause feels risky.

So, Anna moves forward quickly. She isn't making decisions blindly, but she is operating under incomplete information. She trusts the headline metrics and the confidence of the story being told, even as unresolved questions linger in the background. Listening is deferred in favor of forward progress. That choice doesn't explode immediately, but the land mines are being set.

The damage of that missed listening opportunity shows up later, in Act II, as a diffuse but relentless strain on the organization. Integration proves harder than expected. Teams are asked to operate at founder-level intensity to compensate for gaps that were never fully examined. Workloads expand, and ambiguity increases. Leaders respond by pushing harder, moving faster, and demanding higher levels of execution.

What appears to be a sudden breakdown in Act II is actually a delayed consequence. The questions that weren't explored during the acquisition don't disappear. They simply resurface later as firefighting and frustration. Blame begins to fall on teams that are now being asked to deliver miracles in a system built on partial understanding.

The same listening failure repeats internally as Driftwell accelerates its AI transformation. Performance systems remain untouched as review cycles continue based on yesterday's understanding of success. Managers debate rankings even as they privately acknowledge that the work itself has fundamentally changed. Once again, the organization measures output without making sense of what the work now requires.

You see this reflected in Priya's storyline as well. In moments that should have invited inquiry and deliberation, the emphasis was placed on fluency and confidence. Public certainty matters more than personal understanding. Inside teams, people adapt accordingly, reporting execution while internally struggling to make sense of new tools and expectations they were never given time to absorb. Under pressure, listening to these appeals comes across as inefficient. It slows things down and raises uncomfortable questions. And because the system neither rewards nor protects curiosity, listening is ignored.

By Act II, Driftwell is paying compound interest on everything it chose not to hear. The organization keeps moving, but its understanding never catches up. This is how listening fails in modern organizations. Not because leaders don't value it, but because the operating system convinces them they can't afford to pause when things get hard. What feels like progress in the moment becomes fragile over time.

Ownership: When Leaders Stop Owning the Talent Agenda

Ownership blurs at Driftwell when leaders stop owning the human consequences of their decisions. It quickly becomes all business for the non-HR leaders, and that talent burden is placed solely with HR.

In fact, it's the red thread running through Acts I and II for how responsibility for people gets diffused—handed off to process, to HR, to legal, to "the business"—until no one is fully accountable anymore. It becomes incrementally unclear who is responsible for morale, and the people experience.

Anna never explicitly says she doesn't own the talent agenda at Driftwell. In fact, she often speaks as if she does. She invokes commitment and calls for resilience. She asks leaders to step up and drive intensity. But when the moment comes to sit with the real weight of what those words mean, ownership subtly shifts elsewhere. People decisions become HR problems. Layoffs become legal processes, and grief becomes something to be managed rather than held.

As CHRO, James becomes the symbolic owner of humanity in such a system. He is the one expected to explain, absorb, and contain the emotional fallout from decisions made elsewhere. When he asks, "What do I tell the people who built this company?" he is not asking for a script. He is asking for shared ownership of the human cost.

But the operating system doesn't respond with partnership. It responds with delegation. Anna is sharp in that moment and tells James, *Tell them this is how Driftwell survives.*

At that moment, ownership for people transfers. It moves away from the CEO and the leadership team and settles onto HR. And let's be honest, HR often has no real power to shape the decisions that created the pain in the first place. But they are there to pick up the pieces.

This is one of the most common failure safety modes in modern organizations: leaders treat people as a function rather than a responsibility. They speak passionately about talent, culture, and values, but when trade-offs arise, those responsibilities are conveniently assigned to someone else to manage. The operating system reinforces this behavior. It frames people as capacity, roles, and overhead. And it imperceptibly teaches executives that owning the business does not require owning the emotional reality of the people inside it.

Over time, this creates a widening gap in shared reality. Leaders still feel like owners and are compensated as such. They have context, influence, equity, and control over direction. The workforce, meanwhile, is asked to adapt continuously to choices they did not shape and cannot question. They are told to stay committed, even as their sense of belonging and security wears away.

At first, people do try harder. In the short-term, they stretch, overcompensate, and find ways to make it work. They tell themselves it's temporary. But over time, their relationship to the work sours. It's the dynamic that *Office Space* captured so well more than twenty years ago: "*It's not that I'm lazy, it's that I just don't care.*" In modern organizations, you're more likely to hear it translated into safer language: "*That's above my pay grade.*"

It's a rational response to a system that asks people to care deeply without caring for them in return. What's usually maddening to workers is that the operating system still uses the language of ownership—accountability, commitment, resilience—but it no longer places ownership where it belongs: with leaders who have the power to shape conditions. They are asked to trust leaders who have chosen to outsource responsibility for their experience.

Let me be clear. This is not a motivation problem. It's a leadership ownership problem. And once leaders no longer own the human costs of their decisions, not sentimentally, but structurally, no amount of cultural messaging, engagement surveys, or performance incentives can restore what was lost.

Truth: When the System Filters Transparency in All Directions

Truth is the hardest part of the plot to recover once lost. We first see the truth drift downward the moment Anna says, "Draft tight NDAs." Truth breaks at precisely the point where leaders feel most exposed. The instinct isn't to communicate more authentically; it's to contain risk and control the story. What follows is the fallout of that choice. HR and legal teams are stuffing thick manila folders with documents designed to "*sign away the noise*."

That phrase used in the *Strategic Reset* scene—*sign away the noise*—lands hard because it captures the emotional betrayal employees experience in moments like this. Their fear, grief, and confusion are no longer warning signs to heed; they are liabilities to be neutralized. The human response becomes something the system needs to silence.

Truth also thins as it moves upward. Early on, Graham carries what the text describes as a "*nagging fear he didn't want to name*." He sees the cash burn. He worries they overpaid for Priya's company. He knows he needs to bring this to Anna because, as the line tells us, *she deserved honesty*. That sentence matters. It captures the exact moment where truth begins to slip.

Graham is managing two runways at once: the company's financial runway and Anna's emotional one. And he chooses to prioritize Anna's emotions over what's best for the company. As a result, we see Graham delay, hedge, and restrict the flow of information to Anna.

This is what I mean when I say truth is lost both upward and downward. Under pressure, the system doesn't just filter truth to protect the organization from employees. It filters the truth to protect leaders from one another, from the board, and from realities they don't yet feel ready to face.

Once that filtering begins, it becomes self-reinforcing. Less truth ultimately creates less trust. Less trust creates more control, and more control demands even more filtering. That's the loop. Power continues to be restricted to a few, listening deprioritized, ownership diffused, and truth further distorted. And it's one of the most reliable ways organizations lose the plot.

Reclaim Your PLOT

If, when you read this story, you felt a low-key dread—*I've been in a room like that*—that's because Driftwell is running a very common operating system. It's the default OS of modern performance culture: control the permissions, reward speed and output, strip ownership, and filter truth.

Therefore, Act III is not about rejecting systems. It's about rebooting them. It's about leaders learning to realize when their safety mode kicks in and deliberately overriding it. Because regaining the plot at work is about becoming more awake to the invisible code shaping the choices we make under pressure. And once you see that code, you can't unsee it.

This is where an alternative story begins. As you move into Act III, you'll encounter Anna again, but this time she chooses to redistribute power instead of hoarding it. She focuses on listening and rewarding learning instead of just outcomes. Anna reignites ownership by taking full accountability for the human side of business operations. She seeks to rebuild trust by telling the truth, even though it would have been easier not to.

She doesn't do this perfectly, and there are still missteps along the way (we are only human, after all). But she does regain the plot by remaining vigilant over the operating system of organizational behavior when under tension.

What we will learn in Act III is that regaining the plot at work isn't about returning to some idealized past. It's about designing systems that reflect what we now know to be true: people don't need to be controlled to perform. They need to be heard and have shared ownership over what they're building together. This is where our alternative story begins.

Another Way

In the original story, by the time Driftwell's board made its decision, the system had already exerted itself in the only way it knew how. When organizations can no longer surface reality, they will eventually remove the bottleneck. Not always fairly, but this happens predictably. It's why, according to Korn Ferry research, **33% of CEOs don't make it past three years in the role**.[1] Most have experienced drift and operated in a state of organizational delirium by that point.

Anna's CEO exit was framed by the board as swift leadership and by the market as necessary change. A familiar ending for many executives in publicly traded companies today. It's the type of departure most executives recognize, even if they rarely talk about it out loud.

But this does not have to be the way, at least not in this version of the story.

What follows is an alternative reality. One where leadership intervention comes earlier. Before silence hardens into apathy, before profits at all costs cause the team to drift, and the rudderless pursuit of AI leads to delirium.

To be frank, this is not a story about becoming kinder, slower, or less ambitious. It's a story about designing leadership for reality instead of illusion. One of the hardest tasks leaders face is seeing reality as it is—unfiltered, inconvenient, and frequently uncomfortable. Reality demands courage. It requires harder choices, not easier ones. This version of the story asks something different of Anna and of us. It invites us inward, to the moment when a leader chooses truth, even when the stakes are high and the consequences higher.

Scene 1: A Rewiring

Anna had learned, over the years, to keep moving. Speed was her shelter and progress was her proof of competence. If her calendar stayed full and decisions stayed stacked, she could tell herself she was being an effective leader. Slowing down always invited a different question, and one she'd learned to avoid because it never arrived alone.

If I stop pushing, what drops? And if something drops. . . was I ever in control to begin with?

She hadn't always led this way. The pandemic had rewired her internal clock in a way she couldn't undo. Thinking back, it was supposed to just be a few weeks before business returned to normal. But reality presented itself in terms of years, not weeks. During those early pandemic months, options carried real stakes and thin margins.

The fight-or-flight response had been useful then. It had also been addictive.

Even now, years later, she felt most alive chasing the familiar thrill of urgency. It was a hit of adrenaline disguised as purpose.

She noticed it in small things: the way she walked faster than she needed to, the way she treated open space on her calendar like a leak that had to be sealed, the way she'd started using "alignment" as shorthand for "move on." She prided herself on carrying the weight of Driftwell on her shoulders and deep down enjoyed the power that came with that.

That morning, she arrived to find her desk unusually bare.

Over the weekend, she'd finally cleared it. Less for aesthetics, rather her assistant had warned her the board chair would be in her office later that week and "it might help the optics." Anna had thought a bit of chaos on the desk signaled a busy executive, but she still complied.

In the back corner sat a familiar notebook she hadn't opened in years, pressed flat beneath old board packets. She picked it up without intention and flipped through half-formed diagrams and faded notes from a previous version of herself. One who believed systems could be built to support people, not extract from them.

Years ago, Driftwell had tagged her as a high potential. She'd been pulled into an elite leadership accelerator program designed to prepare her for the role she now held. The program required long nights, lost weekends, but afforded her the visibility of being chosen.

Back then, the future felt expansive and exciting. That was before the world became a constant sequence of shocks: policy volatility, cyber threats, inflation, and a market that punished anything that looked like hesitation.

She noticed a particular page. Near the back, one corner folded over, softened from being handled too many times. She read it once. Then again.

It was her own leadership philosophy, drafted after a lecture from General McChrystal she attended while in her leadership program. Principles she'd written to protect herself from the mistakes she'd watched leaders make over and over again. Always promising herself that she would never become one of them.

Anna's non-negotiable leadership principles

- Distributed power is the most effective form of power. Give authority to those closest to the problem.
- Teams that sense stress early survive. Reward cross-functional collaboration and knowledge sharing.
- Success is measured by the health of the whole, over time. Business leadership is a game of chess, not checkers.
- Red team one-way-door decisions. Slow down in order to move fast.
- The truth hurts. Don't lead with thin skin. Keep ego in check; anchor in listening.

She closed the notebook. The ideas hadn't been wrong, but they'd become increasingly inconvenient. It was harder to defend "slow down" in rooms that rewarded certainty and speed. Harder to talk about resilience when investors wanted acceleration. Harder to design systems for truth when control felt like the only lever left.

What unsettled her wasn't that she'd forgotten the principles. It was that somewhere along the way, she'd stopped building the conditions that made them possible. She told herself it was the world. The pace. The board. The market. The endless sequence of urgent things.

And then AI, of course; an entire industry selling the promise that leaders could finally manage complexity without having to sit inside it.

She placed the notebook back on her desk with her leadership non-negotiables page opened. She wanted to keep ruminating on these. Then her eyes wandered to the bookshelf outside her office—the one she kept stocked for any employee bold enough to meander into the executive wing. Most of the leadership classics had been replaced by newer titles. Nearly every spine carried the same promise in bold: AI is here.

She sat back down and turned to her computer screen. An alert blinked on the operations dashboard. Not red, so therefore not urgent. But it was the kind of signal you only catch when you're paying attention.

Scene 2: Heeding the Warning

The warning blinked inside the AI-enabled operations dashboard—one of the first systems she'd approved as CEO. The dashboard was clean and predictive, designed to offer transparency in a company that felt increasingly complex.

Employees had been less enthusiastic. Especially in HR, where roles had been reduced after implementation.

The AI-enabled system analyzed Driftwell's digital exhaust—emails, Slack messages, shared documents. Everything aggregated. Nothing attributable. The model was trained on the behaviors leadership said they valued: collaboration, speed, accountability, resilience.

The blinking alert wasn't red, it was amber and indicated that collaboration was decreasing while all other metrics remained green.

Team Performance Index: <u>Steadily Declining</u>

- Hot Spot: Collaboration Decreasing
- Confidence Level: Moderate **Model Assumes Headcount Remains Stable*

Anna glanced at the clock. She had a board prep call in fifteen minutes. Financial analysts were waiting on updates but that afternoon, James had asked for time to connect.

"Make it ten," Anna said. "High level."

He arrived without slides.

"I want to talk about Ravi and Monica's teams," he said. "Specifically, how they're holding up." Ravi was the new head of engineering and Monica was a long-time Driftwell sales leader.

Anna glanced at the dashboard. "Output is up, what's the problem, James?"

"Yes," James said. "But I don't think the system is surfacing the broken ways we are getting that work done."

She leaned back. "We're in a turnaround. Pressure is expected."

She waited as James looked prepared to deliver news he knew wouldn't make her happy.

"There are two problems with this new AI tool," he said. "First, the sentiment data is getting too positive."

Anna frowned. "Too positive?"

"Yes," he said. "People know they're being monitored. So they've learned what *not* to say where the system can see it."

He continued. "We're seeing *toxic positivity* show up in engagement surveys. Everything sounds fine. Upbeat. Neutral. But it's performative."

"So the AI thinks morale is stable," Anna said.

"Because it's reading filtered responses, not honesty," James replied. "Stress hasn't disappeared, it's just moved elsewhere."

She thought of the dashboard. Mostly green. One amber.

"And the second problem?" she asked.

"The model assumes our talent capacity is fixed," James said. "It treats headcount as stable."

Anna stilled.

"But we know our capacity isn't stable," she said. "We've had attrition in Ravi's group for sure. And we cut part of your team after the rollout." Anna looked away as she said that because she knew how difficult those cuts were for James.

"Yes," James said. "But the AI doesn't see that. That was one of the limitations of the system modeling."

Anna looked back at the alert she'd noticed earlier and read the fine print more carefully.

*Model Assumes Headcount Remains Stable

Assumes.

"So we look healthy," she said slowly, "because people are doing more with less. Which in the short-term, that's part of business, but definitely not a long-term strategy."

James nodded. "And the model doesn't flag it because it's classified as resilience in our dashboard. These AI tools are still fairly new and so once we play with them, we get a better sense of their shortcomings."

The room went quiet. Anna reflected back on her heated argument with James when she approved the new AI tool. He was worried the technology wasn't ready, and that the upside wasn't worth the downside. Anna had dismissed him as being upset about laying off part of his staff. Now, she realized, his instincts might have been right.

"This isn't a recommendation moment. I haven't come up with a solution yet" he said finally. "But it's a listening moment. I'd like to start conducting monthly employee focus groups."

Anna pushed back a bit on this. She worried James might be overreacting and diverting too much energy toward this hunch.

To prove his point, James decided to go there with Anna. "When was the last time someone challenged you in a meeting?" he asked gently.

Anna opened her mouth to speak but then closed it. Meetings had become smoother. Alignment came quickly. She'd taken that as progress.

"I don't know," she said.

"That's what worries me," James replied.

As he stood, he added, "I spend time where the system doesn't look. Anonymous platforms. Glassdoor. Reddit."

"Are we getting dragged?" she asked, defensive now.

"Not exactly," he said. "People vent there so they can stay compliant here."

The moment abruptly interrupted with Anna's phone ringing, meaning the meeting was over. Before picking up the phone, Anna stopped him on his way out of her office. "James, do me a favor and give our vendor this feedback on the AI tool. I am a little worried now that we may have been too bullish on what this tool would actually do for us."

"And James," Anna continued, surprising him. "I want to help you own the outcomes of your focus groups. Please keep me posted as you learn what's really going on."

After her board call, Anna reflected on her sudden irritability. That conversation with James had really gotten under her skin. She thought she had turned around this culture and now it seems her own people were playing her. She didn't like that.

She reopened the dashboard. All green. One amber.

Her attention deviated, not to investors or forecasts for once, but to a post James forwarded along.

"Anna, here is an example of a post, one of many, that makes me think we have a serious culture problem on our hands. It's from an anonymous software engineer:

they say they're not tracking me
but let's see how far your algorithmic reach really goes

i see you reading my emails
in the spirit of efficiency
but it feels a lot like a violation of privacy to me

when is driftwell going to learn
you can't AI your way into my mind

just ask me
i'm not trying to hide
but I will game your system, every time."

She sat with it. She had spent years believing leadership meant carrying the weight alone. Only now did she see how much damage that belief had done.

That night, she opened a blank document and typed a sentence she hadn't allowed herself to write in years: **If high performance depends on people overcompensating, then we are already failing.**

The next morning, she drafted an email about incentives to send to James for input.

> **Subject: Cultural changes in how we think about performance**
>
> Over the past few quarters, we've invested in tools designed to help us see how work is happening across Driftwell. Those tools are doing what they were built to do, but they can only reflect what we choose to value.
>
> Starting next quarter, we are changing how we evaluate leaders. **Outcomes and delivery still matter.** But they will no longer be enough on their own.

50% of leadership bonus will be tied to five observable behaviors:

1. **Escalating risk early** (even when the issue is not fully formed).
2. **Constructive dissent** in decision forums (naming trade-offs, not just problems).
3. **Cross-team capacity sharing** under pressure (and making it visible).
4. **Developing others** (leaving your team stronger, not just busier).
5. **Mentoring and assimilation** of new hires (so success isn't tribal knowledge).

Here's what's changing immediately:

- **Frictionless alignment or last-minute heroics will no longer be treated as hallmarks of high performance.** As a result, we will no longer have our All-Star Award and will move toward a cross-functional award. More soon.
- **Teams will not be penalized for surfacing concerns, uncertainty, or fatigue early.** In fact, we will reward it, because early truth is cheaper than late surprise.

I want to be direct about the why behind this change.

If high performance depends on people overcompensating, then we are already failing.

Over the next few weeks, HR will share what this looks like in performance conversations, including examples of what "good" looks like in different roles.

This is not about lowering the bar.

It's about making sure the bar measures the health of the whole system, not just the endurance of a few individuals.

—Anna

Scene 3: Pursuing Substance, Not Applause

The email went out at 7:12 a.m.

By the time most people opened their laptops, Slack had already lit up with flurries of activity.

The all-hands channel filled quickly as well. James had suggested allowing anonymous posting. Anna had agreed, reluctantly (she'd been working with her coach on allowing decisions to move forward, even if she disagreed).

So is individual recognition gone now? Wonder if we'll still have the All-Star Award?

- *Re:* They better. I gave up my vacation this year to be considered for it.
- *Re:* Same. Feels like a convenient way to cut costs to me.

Does this mean high performance doesn't matter? Feels like we're lowering the bar.

Finally, some mention of teamwork. We've been stuck in silos long enough.

- *Re:* Agreed. Engineering has been brutal this year.
- *Re:* It's not just engineering. Ever since AI performance monitoring rolled out, everything's gotten political. My manager literally told me how to game it.

And cue social loafing. High performers are about to carry even more.

Can't wait for people to argue just to look engaged. Now it's bonus-eligible.

Anna read longer than she meant to.

She'd learned—sometimes the hard way—that incentives were never just transactional mechanisms. They were beliefs with a payroll system. They taught people what was safe to want, what was admired, and what kind of effort counted.

The recognition program hadn't been designed to do harm. It was meant to energize, to focus attention, to make performance visible. But visibility, she was learning, wasn't neutral.

In a system already strained by pace and pressure, recognition had become a spotlight trained on endurance. The people who stayed late. The ones who absorbed chaos without complaining. The ones who made dysfunction look heroic.

They were holding the system together at an average.

She'd seen it before. Attach status or money to a behavior and you don't just reward it, you replicate it. The new AI system hadn't caused this. It had simply reflected back how Driftwell had been operating since the pandemic.

Anna opened a blank email window twice that morning. Once to soften the language. Once to reassure people she hadn't meant *that much* change. She closed both without sending. The hardest part wasn't the backlash. It was resisting the instinct to make it go away.

Graham found her in her office just after noon. She was standing, not sitting, reading Slack on her phone with the screen angled slightly away.

"They're reacting," he said.

"That's one word for it," Anna replied, without looking up.

He closed the door. "We need to talk about how this lands with the board."

She met his eyes. "I assumed we would."

"They're not going to love the language," he said.

"I know."

"But that doesn't mean they won't like the move."

Anna exhaled. "So, how are you framing it?"

"Not as culture. Not as values. Not as trust or humanity," Graham said. "None of that survives the first five minutes."

"Of course it doesn't."

"I'm framing it as a risk correction," he continued. "We've been over-relying on discretionary effort to hit numbers. That's not scalable, and it's not defensible if something breaks."

Anna nodded slowly. "So we're reducing execution fragility."

"Exactly. The system looks strong because a few people are absorbing pressure. This is simply not sustainable."

"They'll ask why now."

"I'll say AI made the culture visible," Graham said. "Not that AI caused the problem. It just exposed the fact that we've been assuming adaptive capacity is infinite."

"And attrition?"

"I'll name it. We may lose some high performers optimized for the old incentives. But keeping them while burning out the system costs more both financially and reputationally."

She studied him. "They'll say this looks like slowing down." The doubt was starting to creep into her voice.

He shrugged. "I'll say it may feel slower at first because we're surfacing work earlier instead of hiding it. The goal isn't fewer ambitions. It's fewer surprises."

"And the stock?"

Graham paused. "Let's see what happens before we start speculating."

Anna was quiet for a moment.

"So you're not pitching this as a transformation."

"No," he said. "I'm pitching it as maintenance. The kind you do before the engine fails."

She nodded. "Good."

"They'll ask if it's reversible."

"And you'll say?"

"That if we're wrong, we'll know sooner than we would have before," he said. "That's the point."

Anna smiled, this time without irony. "Exactly."

As Graham left, she turned back to her screen. The Slack thread was still scrolling with mixed reactions, sharp edges, and real concern.

For the first time, she didn't feel the urge to correct it. She felt the system starting to talk back and it was louder than she expected.

At nine o'clock, Anna walked into the executive meeting without slides.

Priya was already there, composed as usual. James sat beside her, polite, guarded. Ravi and Monica spoke softly at the far end of the table, phones half in hand. Anna had added them to her extended leadership team to gain greater visibility into their business.

All at once, Anna noticed what *wasn't* there. . .

No forced enthusiasm. No pre-meeting buzz. That alone felt like information.

"I assume people are unsettled," Priya said smoothly. "We should be clear that standards aren't changing. We're just evolving how we talk about culture."

Anna felt the instinct flicker, the urge to tidy uncertainty.

"Let's slow down before we decide. . ." Anna said, pausing longer than was comfortable, "I want to hear more about what we might be wrong about."

Priya blinked. "Of course."

"It upset a lot of high performers," Ravi said.

"Yes," Anna replied. "Which tells us something."

"My top sellers are asking if results still matter," Monica said.

"They do," Anna said. "That's why this matters."

She turned to Ravi. "If I reward the person who does the most themselves, what happens?"

"They keep doing more."

"And their team?"

"They wait. Or disengage."

"When we reward the hero," Anna said, "we don't build capacity. We create dependence."

The room went still, not resistant, but alert.

"Higher performance still matters," Priya said carefully.

"I agree," Anna said. "The question is what we're actually measuring, and how many high performers we're unlocking."

She leaned forward.

"Right now, we're using intensity as a proxy for impact. Visibility as a proxy for value. Personal sacrifice as a proxy for leadership."

James felt something release in his chest. He'd been circling this truth for months without language. He was shocked Anna had such articulation for this problem he'd lost sleep over for weeks.

"And when we do that," Anna continued, "we reward people who survive a broken system instead of people who strengthen it."

She placed a single page on the table.

What We Choose to Notice

Three columns:

Strengthening Each Other; Strengthening the System; Strengthening the Customer.

Concrete behaviors listed underneath, argued over with James until midnight. Ravi studied it.

"This is. . . harder."

"Yes," Anna said. "That's intentional."

"How do we measure this?" Priya asked. "I'm used to metrics like lines of code written."

"We don't pretend it's simple," Anna said. "We make it discussable. We train managers to see it. And we stop hiding subjective judgment behind tidy numbers."

"People will say this is vague," Graham said. "Bias even."

"They already do," Anna replied. "We just call it objective because there's a number attached. We all know it isn't."

She knew the room wasn't fully with her. For once, that didn't feel like failure. It felt more like a refinement.

By early afternoon, her calendar filled, not with investors or press, but with employees. She would normally have delegated. She didn't, partly because James pressed for her ownership over the decision.

A senior engineer insisted his contribution was irreplaceable.

A sales director warned they'd lose rainmakers.

An HR partner admitted managers weren't trained to recognize the behaviors Anna was naming.

Anna listened. Every objection was data.

By mid-afternoon, she was exhausted. It reminded her why she'd outsourced culture to HR in the first place. The people side was heavy. Unpredictable. Relentless.

At 3:04 p.m., Ravi emailed:

> *I didn't like this at first. But I think you're right. We've been rewarding the wrong thing.*

At 4:17 p.m., Monica forwarded a resignation from a sales rep:

> *Please accept my 2-week notice. I am leaving for another biotech company. Their bonus structure aligns better with my expectations.*

Anna felt the reflex rise: to explain, to smooth, to control the narrative.

She didn't.

"We're going to lose some people who were excellent at the old system," she said to Graham.

He nodded. "If you're right, we end up with something more resilient."

"And if I'm not?"

"Then we'll know early," he said. "Which is still better than finding out too late."

Anna turned back to the board deck. It would be a harder sell than a reorganization. Harder than a product bet. But for the first time in a long while, she wasn't trying to make it look easy.

Scene 4: Pace Is Political

The pushback didn't arrive all at once.

It showed up in fragments—questions framed as curiosity, calendar invites labeled *urgent*, side comments in meetings that landed just close enough to claim plausible deniability.

Within weeks of retiring the All-Star Award, Driftwell found the next place to test Anna's resolve.

Speed. It always came back to speed.

At the quarterly operating review, Ravi spoke first, as he usually did. Engineering had delivered. Cycle time was down. Defects were flat. The dashboard—recently redesigned with AI-generated insights—glowed reassuringly green.

"We proved we can move fast," Ravi said, tapping the screen. "What my managers are asking now is whether we're about to lose that edge."

Monica jumped in. "Sales is hearing the same thing. Customers don't just want resilience. They want results. They want timelines."

A few heads nodded. Anna waited.

"What they're really asking," Monica continued, "is whether Driftwell still expects urgency or if we're entering a softer phase."

The words landed like a lead balloon.

Anna felt the old instinct rise. The compulsion to reassure. To say *of course not*. To assert she was still decisive, still tough, still worthy of the chair.

Instead, she asked, "What happens to your teams when everything is urgent?"

Monica paused. "They respond."

"For how long?" Anna pressed.

Ravi leaned forward. "Look, no one's arguing for burnout. But let's be honest, some pressure is what separates high performers from everyone else."

Anna nodded. "I agree. Pressure matters."

The room relaxed slightly.

"But pace," she continued, "is not the same as pressure."

That got their attention.

Ravi frowned. "Are you saying we should slow down?"

Anna stood and walked to the whiteboard, aware of how this would look. She could almost hear Graham's voice in her head: *Careful. This is where people decide whether you're operational or theoretical.*

"I'm saying leaders need to stop pretending constant acceleration is sustainable," she said. "Because it isn't. And because pretending it is doesn't make us faster, it just hides where the consequences show up."

She wrote three words on the board.

Acceleration

Sustainment

Recovery

"We're excellent at the first," she said, circling *Acceleration*. "And we've mistaken it for the whole job."

Ravi crossed his arms. "Our competitors aren't running recovery cycles."

"No," Anna replied. "They're running attrition cycles. I know because many of their leaders have recently reached out asking to come here."

The room fell silent.

Graham glanced at the dashboard. "The AI projections show we can maintain current output for another two quarters," he said carefully. "Assuming attrition stays flat."

Anna wrote and underlined the word on the board.

Assuming

"And what happens if it doesn't?" she asked.

No one answered immediately. They all knew the model's blind spot now.

"When leaders say 'move faster,'" Anna continued, "they're not just setting a timeline. They're deciding who pays the price. And it's almost never the people in this room."

Monica frowned. "So what's the alternative? We tell customers to wait while competitors eat our lunch?"

Anna shook her head.

"We tell the truth. And we design the work around it."

Acceleration would be explicit, time-bound, and owned. Recovery would be planned, not implied. AI tools would be used to remove low-value work, not compress judgment into smaller windows. Leaders would be evaluated not just on output, but on whether their teams could sustain it without heroics.

Ravi exhaled. "That's. . . complicated."

"Yes," Anna said. "So is reality."

Priya, who had been uncharacteristically subdued, finally spoke. "What worries me is that people will hear this as permission to do less."

Anna looked at her. "That's only true if we believe effort is the only thing holding performance together."

The sentence seemed harsher than Anna intended, but she saw the concept register for the team.

A week later, the theory met its test.

A major customer escalated, demanding a delivery timeline that would compress a month of work into ten days. The old playbook was familiar to all: rally, push, absorb the damage.

The room waited for Anna's call. Instead, she asked a question, "What breaks if we say no?"

"We risk losing them," Ravi said emphatically.

"And if we say yes?" Anna asked.

James answered. "We borrow against teams that are already stretched. Attrition risk spikes, again."

Anna closed her eyes briefly. She knew this was the moment that would get remembered—by the board, by Sales, by her own team.

"We counter," she said. "With a timeline we can actually sustain."

Monica stiffened. "They won't like it."

"I know."

The customer pushed back. Hard. The deal went to the brink. Monica fought for a compromise and secured a timeline that was still aggressive, but survivable.

Revenue slipped that quarter. Not catastrophically, but enough to get noticed. Two managers told Anna privately she was making Driftwell "less competitive."

And yet, something else happened in parallel.

Teams stopped hiding exhaustion. Managers planned work instead of improvising. Problems surfaced earlier and when they were cheaper to solve. The pace changed and reflected a truer delivery cycle.

Weeks later, Monica forwarded an email from the customer.

The quality of this delivery was higher than expected. Let's keep working together to find a way to achieve this consistently.

Anna read it once, then set her phone down. This wasn't a headline, but it was an indication that the operating system was no longer running on borrowed energy. And for the first time since she'd taken the role, Anna felt it moving under its own power.

Scene 5: Interdependence Hurts

The problem didn't present itself as resistance, it shrouded itself as efficiency.

Six months after the changes to incentives and pace, Driftwell's teams began doing what they'd always done when pressure mounted: protect themselves.

Engineering eventually stopped lending senior talent to Product. Sales escalated customer requests directly to executives again, bypassing cross-functional planning. HR noticed a spike in "urgent exceptions."

Anna first felt the tone during a routine cross-functional review. The agenda was tight. The cadence was professional. The updates were clean. A little too clean.

Ravi walked through engineering KPIs with confidence. Monica shared strong pipeline numbers. Priya outlined an ambitious roadmap, framed carefully around what her team could control.

Anna listened and felt the absence of productive tension.

"Can we pause?" she asked.

"I'm hearing a lot about local success," she said, "but very little about shared dependency."

Ravi frowned slightly. "We've been trying to reduce dependencies. To remain efficient."

Anna turned to Priya. "Your roadmap assumes engineering capacity Ravi hasn't committed to. Is that right?"

Priya hesitated, just a fraction too long. "We're optimizing around what's within our control."

The phrase was used like a shield. James shifted in his seat. He'd seen the anonymous comments. He knew there was an undercurrent of frustration between Priya's AI team and Ravi's engineers that had been building for weeks.

"Optimizing locally often looks responsible," Anna said slowly. "Until the system needs something else."

Ravi leaned forward. "With respect, we've been burned before. We share capacity, timelines slip, and engineering takes the hit."

Monica nodded. "Same. When deals fall apart, Sales owns the fallout. Interdependence sounds nice until someone has to explain the miss."

There it was.

Not resistance to collaboration, but resistance to exposure.

"What happens to Driftwell if everyone is right to protect themselves?" Anna asked.

No one answered.

Finally, Graham spoke. "We get efficient silos," he said. "Which works until it doesn't."

Anna nodded. "Interdependence is uncomfortable," she said. "It makes risk visible. It forces negotiation. It makes performance harder to attribute."

She paused. "Which is exactly why leadership either shows up here or it disappears. It's non-negotiable for me."

After the meeting, the emails started.

From Ravi:

> *I can't keep lending my strongest people into chaos. Priya needs more operational discipline before I'm comfortable with this approach.*

From Monica:

> *Sales is already carrying enough risk. Cooperation without protection isn't sustainable.*

The message was clear. Teams were refusing to be vulnerable without cover.

That night, Anna created a sketch. Not as an organizational chart, but as a systems analysis, a course she had taken back in graduate school. It made visible the interactions and where work stalled. Where decisions bottlenecked. Where blame accumulated.

By morning, she made a move that surprised everyone. She canceled the weekly ELT meeting. In its place, she launched a rotating forum of mid-level leaders from across functions. No polished decks or planned updates. One rule: you bring one dependency you're currently hiding.

The first session was tense. People spoke carefully, eyes darting, testing for consequences.

A senior engineer went first. "We stopped supporting Product because when the roadmap changes last minute, we're the ones who look incompetent."

A sales leader followed. "We bypass Planning because when deals slip, no one asks what broke upstream."

An HR manager added, "We see burnout forming, but we're afraid to escalate without evidence."

The room exhaled together.

When Anna joined the third session, not to lead, but to listen, the truth accelerated.

She didn't defend. She didn't fix. She didn't promise protection she couldn't give. Instead, she made it structural. People weren't the problem here, her system was.

Executive bonuses were now tied, not to individual metrics, but to cross-team outcomes. Leaders had to name what they were borrowing from the system and what they were returning. Dependencies became visible, negotiable, legitimate.

AI tools were repurposed—this time to map work flowing between teams instead of measuring individual delivery. Bottlenecks appeared in places no one had wanted to name.

Some leaders bristled.

"You're asking us to give up control," one director said flatly.

Anna didn't argue. "I'm asking you to give up the illusion of it."

Not everyone stayed.

A handful of leaders who'd built influence on gatekeeping exited over the next quarter. They weren't bad actors. They simply preferred systems where success could be individually retained, not shared.

The organization downshifted briefly, but then it stabilized.

Fewer surprises made it to the executive level—not because people were hiding them, but because fewer dependencies were being hidden. Teams borrowed talent and returned it. Conversations got messier and responsibility got clearer.

One afternoon, James stopped by Anna's office.

"This is the first place I've worked where people admit they need each other," he said.

Anna smiled faintly. "That's not culture," she said. "That's design. And you are a big reason we've been able to make this shift."

James smiled, finally feeling seen for his many sleepless nights. As he left, she glanced at the system map pinned to her wall. It was untidy, lines crossed and arrows doubled back, but it was reality.

Interdependence hadn't made Driftwell slower, it made vulnerabilities visible. And for the first time, visibility was a welcome change.

Scene 6: AI as a Mirror

The boardroom had better coffee than the rest of the building. Anna noticed it every time—the heavier cups, the darker beans, it was definitely Italian roast.

She arrived early, setting her notebook beside a thin stack of printed pages. No deck. No special animations. Just numbers and a final page labeled **Model Assumptions**.

Graham took the seat next to her.

"They're frustrated," he said under his breath.

Anna nodded. "They paid for efficiency."

Marcus opened the meeting without ceremony.

"We made a significant bet on AI," he said. "Automation, forecasting, decision support. The promise was leverage. So far, the leverage isn't showing up."

Before Anna could respond, one of the directors leaned forward. Tom. Former operator. Sharp, impatient, and openly skeptical of anything that sounded like process.

"I don't understand why this is hard," Tom said. "AI doesn't get tired. It doesn't need training. The whole point was to *remove* friction and headcount."

A few heads nodded.

"If we're still talking about capacity," he continued, "then something isn't working."

Anna slid the first page across the table.

"This is Driftwell measured traditionally," she said. "Productivity is up. Cycle times are holding. On paper, the investment looks fine."

Tom barely glanced at it.

"Then why aren't we moving faster?"

Anna slid the second page forward.

"This is Driftwell measured as a system."

The room leaned in.

Rework rates spiking late. Decision reversals after execution had already begun. Attrition risk concentrated in a handful of roles—the same ones mediating between AI outputs and human judgment.

"These patterns existed before AI," Anna said. "What's changed is that we can see them clearly now."

Tom frowned. "So the technology works."

"Yes," Anna said.

"Then why are you asking for more people?"

There it was.

"Because AI doesn't eliminate judgment," Anna replied. "It concentrates it."

Tom shook his head. "That's not what we bought."

"What we bought," Anna said evenly, "was speed. What we didn't fund was the capability required to use that speed responsibly."

Another director cut in. "Are you saying the teams can't keep up?"

"I'm saying they are keeping up," Anna replied. "By absorbing the cost."

She tapped the page.

"AI assumes capacity is stable. That assumption only holds if the same people can carry more complexity, more exceptions, more decisions—without breaking."

Tom crossed his arms. "Then push the system harder. That's the point of leverage."

"And when it breaks?" Anna asked.

He didn't hesitate. "Then we adjust."

The room fell silent.

"So, let me get this straight," Tom said. "We invested in AI to reduce dependency on people. Now you're telling us we need to hire more of them?"

"I'm telling you," Anna said, "that AI scales whatever system it's embedded in. Right now, it's scaling a fragile system."

Marcus leaned forward. "What exactly are you proposing?"

Anna didn't back down.

"Targeted investment in the roles where decision-making sits. Training. Coverage. Some slack. Enough capacity so AI actually improves outcomes instead of just accelerating them."

Tom let out a short laugh. "That delays the upside."

"No," Anna said. "It protects it."

He shook his head. "This is a misread. If AI needs this much human support, then it's not delivering what we paid for."

"That's a fair conclusion," Anna said. "Or we could acknowledge that *the value of AI depends on people's ability to use it effectively*. And we haven't invested enough on the people-side of this."

Marcus looked around the table.

"I'm hearing two positions," he said. "One says double down on efficiency. The other says slow down to stabilize."

Tom met Marcus's eye. "We didn't invest to stand still."

A pause.

Marcus nodded. "We proceed as planned."

The decision landed neatly. No drama. No vote.

Anna felt it in her chest anyway.

The meeting moved on.

Outside the boardroom, Graham exhaled.

"They went with him," he said.

Anna nodded. "I know."

"And you're okay with that?"

She thought for a moment.

"They didn't disagree with the data," she said. "They disagreed with the patience."

"And if they're right?"

"Then the system will reward speed," Anna said.

"And if you're right?"

She looked back through the glass, at the now empty chairs and untouched coffee.

"Then it will tell us, later than it should."

Graham frowned. "That's not much of a win."

Anna picked up her notebook.

"It's not a win," she said. "But it was dialogue."

Scene 7: The Unsexy Win

A year later, the world reminded Driftwell it was not done testing them. The alert came in before dawn.

A key supplier in Eastern Europe had halted shipments indefinitely after overnight sanctions were announced. Borders were closing. Freight contracts were being voided mid-route. Within minutes, industry Slack channels lit up with speculation and panic. Analysts began drafting notes. Customers started asking questions that didn't yet have answers.

In the old Driftwell, this would have triggered a familiar cascade of events: an emergency executive meeting. Dozens of frantic emails. Leaders stepping in to "own" the problem. Teams working late into the night to compensate for decisions that arrived too late.

Anna's phone buzzed. She hadn't rushed to the office and instead took a minute to make her own favorite coffee.

By the time she arrived, the system was humming.

Engineering had flagged which products were most exposed. Procurement had surfaced alternative suppliers—not as a scramble, but as options already mapped. Sales had paused outreach to affected customers, not to spin, but to buy time. AI dashboards showed strain in specific areas but not generalized alarm.

The issues were being localized.

At the cross-functional review, no one raised their voice. In the midst of the chaos, the workforce exhibited a calmness Anna hadn't seen before at Driftwell.

"This will negatively impact one release," Ravi said. "Not the whole roadmap. Let's keep that into perspective as we react today."

"We'll need to renegotiate timelines with three customers," Monica added. "Not all of them."

James spoke next. "Teams are stretched, but not overcompensating yet. If we move work now, we avoid it."

Anna listened. No one looked at her for permission. They were looking at one another.

"What do you need from me?" she finally asked.

There was a pause because the question wasn't performative anymore.

"Cover, to be honest," Monica said. "Alignment of priorities," Ravi added. "And air," James said simply. "So people don't panic."

Anna nodded. "You have it. I will get an all-company email out today. Monica and Ravi, I will keep spots open on my calendar today for proactive check-ins."

But the disruption lasted weeks, not days. Anna's calendar was upside down longer than she anticipated.

There were tense conversations with customers. One contract was lost. The stock dipped slightly, then leveled off. The news cycle moved on, as it always did.

Inside Driftwell, something else happened. The problem didn't metastasize. No one burned out heroically. No one pretended the system was fine when it wasn't. Work adjusted. Trade-offs were named and recovery was planned, not improvised. Teammates used language like, "I'm going to sprint for the next week, can I plan on you stepping in while I take a day to recover."

AI flagged where strain was increasing, and leaders responded before it turned into suppression. The system was actually flexing.

On an ordinary Tuesday not long after, Anna walked the floor. People were working. Talking. Some even disagreeing. Others were asking for help without apology. Meetings ended on time. Some weeks were fast. Others were deliberately slower.

The adrenaline was gone and with it the constant bracing.

James stopped by her office in the late afternoon.

"You know," he said, "this supply chain disruption would've broken us a year ago."

Anna looked up. "What made the difference?"

He thought for a moment. "No one hesitated to raise flags and everyone stepped up to figure out how to help."

Down the hall, Priya was in a working session running a customer focus group. Her weekly coaching had taught her that her superpower wasn't intensity, but listening. She was asking better questions than she used to. Letting others shape the answer.

Graham brought the latest numbers later that evening. They were unremarkable.

Margins held. Costs were controlled. Recovery timelines were realistic. No thrilling rebound, but also no collapse. Stable sustainable performance in a down market.

That night, as she left the building, the parking lot was half full. She would once have judged this as an unmotivated workforce, instead she recognized it as a balanced workforce. It was Friday evening, after all.

The world outside was still loud. Still volatile and still unforgiving. But Driftwell was resolute and able to sustain itself.

Leadership hadn't become easier for Anna, but it had become more honest. Decisions were shared, listening was prioritized, truth traveled faster, and people were no longer someone else's problem. Her system, that had taken a couple of years to get right, had just been tested, and to her amusement, felt stronger.

Epilogue: Ten Years Later

Anna hadn't expected to still be here.

Statistically, she shouldn't have been. The average tenure of a CEO in her industry barely stretched past three years, and Driftwell had lived through more volatility than most. There were quarters she was praised for holding the line, and others when critics wondered aloud whether restraint had become hesitation. Growth slowed, then stabilized. Talent churned, then settled. The pull toward delirium never fully disappeared, but it never took over either.

That, Anna had come to believe, was the work.

Driftwell didn't become legendary under her leadership. It became steadier, more humane, and stronger with time. Less impressive in headlines, perhaps, but more durable in ways that didn't show up neatly on earnings calls.

Anna never made the front cover of *Forbes*, as she once dreamed she would, but she became highly regarded in the industry. She recently received a lifetime achievement award at her field's leading conference, and she'd be lying if she said she didn't appreciate the recognition. Over the years, she'd become a source of counsel for many of her peers, who admired her steadiness and her ability to keep Driftwell stable through recent market downturns.

Now, at sixty-two, Anna sat at the same desk she'd occupied for a decade, reviewing succession plans instead of strategy decks. Retirement hovered closer than she liked to admit. Not because she was tired, exactly, but because she knew when staying too long became its own kind of drift.

Leadership, after all, wasn't about being indispensable. It was about leaving behind something that could survive without you.

The list in front of her was short. The board wanted certainty. The markets always did. And the world—once again—was unraveling faster than anyone had predicted. The alert had come that morning.

A major AI breakthrough thanks to developments in quantum computing: one that collapsed development timelines overnight and rendered entire operating models obsolete. At the same time, escalating geopolitical tensions had tipped toward open conflict. Supply chains were already reacting. Capital was skittish. Governments were invoking emergency powers. Every system Driftwell depended on was about to be stress-tested at once.

Anna closed the report and leaned back.

This wasn't just disruption. This was the kind of moment that revealed what an organization was actually built for.

She immediately thought about Priya as a potential candidate for her seat. Everyone did.

Priya had risen quickly—brilliant, articulate, unflinchingly composed. Priya didn't resist the coaching, instead actively embraced new leadership behaviors. Her more approachable style, coupled with her deep understanding of the new AI architectures, made her a shoo-in. Investors trusted her, the board admired her, and analysts had already begun to speculate.

Priya would move fast though. She operated in that acceleration mode more than Anna thought necessary. But she would keep Driftwell competitive. She would not be sentimental, but Anna didn't doubt her competence for a second.

What she wasn't sure of, what no model could predict, was how Priya would hold the human system once the pressure spiked. When fear returned and shortcuts became tempting. When efficiency demanded sacrifices no slide deck ever named explicitly. She still leveraged her own executive coach, who warned Anna that Priya needed a balanced counterpart to keep her in check if she were to get the CEO position.

But there was also a different option. A less obvious one—not someone already being groomed for the job.

This other leader didn't command rooms, but listened to them. They were the person employees sought out after hard meetings for grounding. They noticed when teams were running hot long before burnout appeared in the data. They had an almost inconvenient habit of asking why, just as everyone else was eager to move on to how fast.

They were intentional. This person believed that in moments of chaos, the instinct to accelerate was often the very thing that caused organizations to lose their way. That speed without sense-making wasn't progress, it was drift.

This leader would most definitely frustrate the board. Struggle to fit their instincts into a slide. They would insist that trust, once broken, took longer to rebuild than any product roadmap allowed. But the people within the system would benefit.

Anna placed the two profiles side by side.

It would be easier, she knew, to recommend Priya. The world rewarded leaders who moved quickly in moments like this.

But Anna had learned something over the years—something no leadership book had ever prepared her for. The greatest risk wasn't choosing the wrong successor. It was designing a system so fragile that only one kind of leader could survive it.

She thought back to the early days, when Driftwell had flirted with delirium. When speed, data, and complexity drowned out her own discernment. When humanity had been treated as a liability instead of a stabilizing force. It had taken years to pull the organization back from that edge.

The question now wasn't whether Driftwell could withstand another shock. It was whether it had learned enough to continue to avoid the drift, no matter who sat in her chair.

Anna closed the folder.

Soon, she would have to make her final recommendation. Soon, the board would decide. Soon, Driftwell would belong to someone else.

But for a moment longer, she allowed herself to sit with the question she knew mattered most, and one she could no longer answer alone.

When the world accelerates toward chaos, do you choose the leader who can move fastest or the one who knows what must not be rushed?

This was the choice she had to make.

Notes

Introduction: Why the Future of Leadership Speaks in Stories, Not Data

1. I define humanity in this book as the essential set of qualities that make us fully human and distinct from technologies, including empathy, dignity, compassion, curiosity, and the ability to connect and care for one another.
2. LinkedIn News. "Fewer Workers Want to Be Managers." *LinkedIn.* Accessed November 18, 2025. https://www.linkedin.com/news/story/fewer-workers-want-to-be-managers-6636596.
3. Deming, W. Edwards. *Out of the Crisis.* Cambridge, MA: Massachusetts Institute of Technology, Center for Advanced Engineering Study, 1982.

Prelude: The Urgent Meeting

1. 996 refers to a work schedule common in parts of the tech industry, meaning 9 a.m. to 9 p.m., six days a week. It represents a seventy-two-hour working week that has become an informal (and controversial) standard in some organizations, particularly in East Asian and Silicon Valley-influenced tech cultures.

ACT I: The Drift

1. Taylor, Frederick Winslow. *The Principles of Scientific Management.* New York: Harper & Brothers, 1911.
2. Marwell, Gerald, and Ruth E. Ames. "Economists Free Ride, Does Anyone Else? Experiments on the Provision of Public Goods, IV." *Journal of Public Economics* 15, no. 3 (1981): 295–310.

3. Carter, John R., and Michael D. Irons. "Are Economists Different, and If So, Why?" *Journal of Economic Perspectives* 5, no. 2 (1991): 171–177.
4. Liberman, Varda, Steven M. Samuels, and Lee Ross. "The Name of the Game: Predictive Power of Reputations Versus Situational Labels in Determining Prisoner's Dilemma Choices." *Personality and Social Psychology Bulletin* 30, no. 9 (2004): 1175–1185.
5. Mills, C. Wright. "Situated Actions and Vocabularies of Motive." *American Sociological Review* 5, no. 6 (1940): 904–913.
6. Wheatley, Margaret J. 2017. *Who Do We Choose to Be? Facing Reality, Claiming Leadership, Restoring Sanity*. Oakland, CA: Berrett-Koehler Publishers.
7. Ernst & Young. "How Businesses Can Stand the Test of Time." EY Insights (June 16, 2023). https://www.ey.com/en_gl/insights/consulting/how-businesses-can-stand-the-test-of-time.
8. Friedman, Milton. "The Social Responsibility of Business Is to Increase Its Profits." *The New York Times Magazine* (September 13, 1970).
9. Phillips, Matt. "The Rich Now Own a Record Share of Stocks." *Axios* (January 10, 2024). Accessed November 18, 2025. https://www.axios.com/2024/01/10/wealthy-own-record-share-stock-market.
10. Jensen, Michael C., and William H. Meckling. "Theory of the Firm: Managerial Behavior, Agency Costs and Ownership Structure." *Journal of Financial Economics* 3, no. 4 (October 1976): 305–360. https://doi.org/10.1016/0304-405X(76)90026-X.
11. Economic Policy Institute. "CEO Pay Has Grown 1,094% Since 1978, While Typical Worker Compensation Rose Only 26%" (September 27, 2024). https://www.epi.org/publication/ceo-pay-in-2023/.
12. Donaldson, Thomas, and James P. Walsh. "Toward a Theory of Business." *Research in Organizational Behavior* 35 (2015): 181–207. https://doi.org/10.1016/j.riob.2015.10.002.
13. Monahan, Kelly. *How Behavioral Economics Influences Management Decision-Making: A New Paradigm*. London: Academic Press, 2018. See Section 2.5.6, "An Alternative Purpose of the Firm Debated Throughout the 20th Century."
14. Accenture. *360° Value Report 2024*. Accenture plc. 2024. https://www.accenture.com/content/dam/accenture/final/accenture.com/a-com-custom-component/iconic/document/360°-Value-Report-2024-Custom-1-20.pdf.
15. Gallup Inc. "Element 8: Mission or Purpose." *Gallup Workplace* (February 5, 2021). Accessed November 18, 2025. https://www.gallup.com/topic/element-8-mission-or-purpose.aspx.
16. Ferry, Korn. 2024. *Motivation Meter: Employee Motivation Hits Lowest Level Since 2019*. Korn Ferry Institute. https://www.kornferry.com/insights/articles/motivation-meter-2024.

17. Galinsky, Adam D., Joe C. Magee, M. Ena Inesi, and Deborah H. Gruenfeld. "Power and Perspectives Not Taken." *Psychological Science* 17, no. 12 (2006): 1068–1074.
18. Fast, Nathanael J., Ethan R. Burris, and Caroline A. Bartel. "Managing to Stay in the Dark: Managerial Self-Efficacy, Ego Defensiveness, and the Aversion to Employee Voice." *Academy of Management Journal* 57, no. 4 (2014): 1013–1034.
19. Keltner, Dacher. *The Power Paradox: How We Gain and Lose Influence*. New York: Penguin Press, 2016.
20. Keltner, Dacher, Deborah H. Gruenfeld, and Cameron Anderson. "Power, Approach, and Inhibition." *Psychological Review* 110, no. 2 (2003): 265–284.
21. Gallup. *State of the Global Workplace: 2024 Report*. Washington, D.C.: Gallup, 2024.
22. Ito, Ki, "How Much Is Corporate Loyalty Worth to You?" *Business Insider* (September 29, 2025). https://www.businessinsider.com/employee-employer-loyalty-workplace-take-lower-careers-2025-9.
23. Ito, Aki, "A Skeptic and an Optimist Discuss Loyalty in the Workplace," *Business Insider* (October 20, 2025). https://www.businessinsider.com/debate-over-workplace-loyalty-2025-10.
24. von Wachter, Till M., Jae Song, and Joyce Manchester. "Long-Term Earnings Losses Due to Mass Layoffs During the 1982 Recession: An Analysis Using U.S. Administrative Data from 1974 to 2008." *American Economic Review* 99, no. 2 (May 2009): 569–573.
25. Cascio, Wayne F. "Downsizing: What Do We Know? What Have We Learned?" *Academy of Management Perspectives* 7, no. 1 (1993): 95–104.

ACT II: The Delirium

1. Lichtenberg, Nick. "Scott Galloway Warns of 'Nowhere to Hide' in Markets if the OpenAI Story Unravels." *Fortune* (November 10, 2025). https://fortune.com/2025/11/10/scott-galloway-nowhere-to-hide-ai-bubble-sam-altman.
2. Upwork Research Institute. *From Burnout to Balance: AI-Enhanced Work Models for the Future*. Upwork, 2025. https://www.upwork.com/research/ai-enhanced-work-models.
3. U.S. Bureau of Labor Statistics. "Employment and Unemployment Among Youth," August 2025.
4. Ceniza-Levine, Caroline. "Gen Z Prefers Advice from ChatGPT over Managers—How to Make Career Development a Competitive Advantage." *Forbes* (February 13, 2024). https://www.forbes.com/sites/carolinecenizalevine/2024/02/13/gen-z-prefers-advice-from-chatgpt-

over-managers-how-to-make-career-development-a-competitive-advantage/.

5. The Upwork Research Institute. "Freelancing Meets Gen Z Modern Work Needs." May 14, 2024. https://www.upwork.com/research/gen-z-work-requirements.
6. Deloitte. *The Deloitte Global 2023 Gen Z and Millennial Survey*. London: Deloitte, 2023.
7. Gallup. *State of the Global Workplace 2024 Report*. Washington, D.C.: Gallup, 2024.
8. Mishel, Lawrence and Jori Kandra, *CEO Pay Has Skyrocketed 1,322 Percent Since 1978*. Washington, D.C.: Economic Policy Institute, 2021. https://www.epi.org/publication/ceo-pay-in-2020/.
9. Deloitte. "Stress and Anxiety Have Changed but Still Remain for Gen Zs and Millennials." Insights2Action™ (June 9, 2023).
10. Edelman. *2025 Edelman Trust Barometer: Reversing the Descent into Grievance*. New York: Edelman, 2025. https://www.edelman.com/trust/2025/Trust-Barometer/reversing-descent-grievance.

ACT III: The Dream: Reclaiming the Plot

1. Korn Ferry. "The Three-Year Itch." *Korn Ferry Insights* (accessed March 15, 2026). https://www.kornferry.com/insights/briefings-for-the-board room/the-three-year-itch.

About the Author

Dr. Kelly Monahan is a globally respected leader in the future of work, whose career has been dedicated to helping organizations thrive amid technological disruption, shifting talent dynamics, and economic uncertainty. As a former tech research executive, she led Future of Work at Meta and served as Founder and Managing Director of Upwork's Future of Work Research Institute, partnering with senior executives to apply cutting-edge insights to workforce strategy, organizational design, and leadership transformation. Her research has shaped how some of the world's most influential companies understand distributed work, talent development, and the human experience at work.

As an international keynote speaker, Monahan introduces audiences to the human side of workplace evolution. Drawing on firsthand research, she explores the trends shaping how we work today and what lies ahead, equipping decision-makers with the insights, tools, and resources needed to better understand and support their employees.

She highlights key data that informs more effective people-related decision-making and examines the role of technology as organizations rethink their talent strategies. Grounded in an unshakeable belief in human potential, Monahan's people-first approach helps organizations design more purposeful and meaningful workplace experiences.

Prior to joining Big Tech, Monahan served as Principal Director of Global Talent Research at Accenture and was the lead future-of-work researcher at Deloitte. Earlier roles across human resources, analytics, and media strategy give her a holistic understanding of how people, technology, and business systems must evolve together to shape the future.

Today, as the founder of Beyond the Desk, Monahan brings world-class research and cross-industry insights directly to leaders navigating the next era of work. She equips executives with evidence-based guidance on harnessing AI responsibly, redefining talent needs, and building resilient, human-centered organizations in a rapidly shifting economic landscape. With a background spanning behavioral science, technology, and global workforce strategy, she translates complex trends into clear, actionable strategies that empower leaders to make confident decisions amid uncertainty.

An expert whose daily work is laying the foundation for a future of work that works, Monahan has been recognized and published in both applied and academic journals, including *Harvard Business Review*, *MIT Sloan Management Review*, and *Journal of Strategic Management*. She is the author of the best-selling leadership book *Essential* (Wiley, 2025), has written more than two dozen publications, is a TEDx speaker, and is frequently quoted in the media on talent decision-making and other aspects of the future of work. She has recently appeared on Bloomberg, WSJ, CNBC and Forbes.

Acknowledgments

First and foremost, thank you to **Kim Fazio**. There would be no *Reclaim the Plot* without you. Thank you for being there every step of the way and for bringing your invaluable coaching expertise to this work. I am so excited for the world to experience your Coaching Corners and deeply grateful for your endless support throughout this project. You are the best co-conspirator a person could ask for.

To the early readers who offered such valuable feedback and insight: thank you. **General McChrystal**, your early endorsement gave me the momentum and confidence to think bigger about this book. Your work helping leaders empower their teams has been a meaningful foundation for my own research and writing. **Alexis Fink**, thank you for the essential leadership you brought while we worked together at Meta, and for the example you continue to set for leaders reclaiming the plot today. I so appreciated your early feedback on the manuscript. **Jeremy Watson**, you were one of the first readers of this manuscript, and your feedback helped clarify important areas for improvement, including the title. Thank you for sharing your coaching expertise and helping make this book stronger. **Eva Sage-Gavin**, thank you for being a voice of reason and for representing the executive audience so thoughtfully as an early reader. Your time, guidance, and belief in me have meant the world. You are the kind of leader I hope to become.

Anna Brown, thank you for being an early champion of this book and for listening to its origin story in its earliest days. Your support, encouragement, and belief in the idea long before it became a reality meant more than you know.

Michelle Sawa, you have been a godsend from the beginning. We have been through the trenches together, and I am so thankful for your support and your early read of this manuscript. **Lisa Sun**, I am grateful our paths crossed when they did, and so appreciative of your early support for this project. Thank you for being one of its earliest champions. **Lindsay Shookus**, thank you for taking the time to read this work and for bringing your producer's perspective to it. Your early support and feedback meant so much. **Neen James**, thank you for reading early and for connecting me with your network to help this book shine in the marketplace. **Jen Fisher**, thank you for being such a great leader, from our time together at Deloitte to your early support of *Reclaim the Plot*. I am so honored to be in your orbit. **Christie Smith**, thank you for paving the way with *Essential*, which made it possible for me to write this next book. I am deeply grateful for your belief in me and your unwavering support.

To the **Wiley team**: **Alison Bohn**, you have been exactly the editor I needed for this work. I am so grateful for your advocacy, your belief in the book, and the care you brought to it. I am thrilled we had the opportunity to partner on this project. **Zach Schisgal**, thank you for believing in *Essential* and for taking a chance on this next project. **Sunnye Collins**, your editorial eye and thoughtful feedback made this manuscript even better. You are one of the best. **Michelle Hacker**, thank you for your early problem-solving as we colored outside the lines with the manuscript and format. I so appreciate your support, your vision for this work, and the way you helped bring it to life on the page.

To **Mat Miller, Peter Knox, Brian Morrison, Alana Whitman, and the rest of the Book Highlight team**: I am so glad we had the chance to partner again on this book launch and find creative ways to bring this story to market. Your early belief in and excitement about this book gave me the confidence to think more boldly about the fictional company and characters. Thank you for your partnership and tireless support.

To my team at **Leading Authorities**, thank you for championing this book project. **Bryn Doubledee**, thank you for connecting me with so many exceptional keynote speakers who became not only champions of this book, but also friends along the way. And to all of my clients, thank you for trusting me to come into your organizations and for engaging with early previews of this work. In particular, thank you to **Thasunda Brown Duckett, Claire Borelli, Nneka Chiazor, Julie Lodge-Jarrett**, **Mike Dominguez, Matthew Upchurch**, and the many other executives who are reclaiming the plot in their organizations.

Thank you to **Black Tie Media**, **Frisco Chavez**, and **Ryan Mellinger** for capturing early readings of the manuscript and bringing its themes and characters to life through inspiring media.

Shannon Monahan, thank you for being one of the constants in my life. No matter where life has taken us, you've always been a source of support, perspective, laughter, and love. I am endlessly grateful for your encouragement.

Finally, thank you to my nephews, **Lincoln and Dean**, who inspire me every day to reclaim the plot for the next generation of workers.

Index

It's Time to Reclaim Your Plot

With resources and support beyond the book, including:

Book Discussion Guide
The P-L-O-T Framework
The Repair Pathway
Reflection Exercises
Video + Media
Speaking
Workshops
and more!

ReclaimThePlotBook.com